50 Top Tips
for Managing Behaviour

D0420078

CP035182

CORNWALL COLLEGE

A Speechmark Practical Resource

50 Top Tips

for Managing Behaviour

Dave Stott

Speechmark

www.speechmark.net

Published by
Speechmark Publishing Ltd, 70 Alston Drive, Bradwell Abbey,
Milton Keynes MK13 9HG, UK
Tel: +44 (0)1908 326944   Fax: +44 (0)1908 326960
www.speechmark.net

First published 2009

Copyright © Dave Stott 2009

Illustrations copyright © Bill Stott

All rights reserved. The whole of this work, including all text and illustrations, is protected by copyright. No part of it may be copied, altered, adapted or otherwise exploited in any way without express prior permission, unless it is in accordance with the provisions of the Copyright Designs and Patents Act 1988 or in order to photocopy or make duplicating masters of those pages so indicated, without alteration and including copyright notices, for the express purposes of instruction and examination. No parts of this work may otherwise be loaded, stored, manipulated, reproduced, or transmitted in any form or by any means, electronic or mechanical, including photocopying and recording, or by any information, storage and retrieval system without prior written permission from the publisher, on behalf of the copyright owner.

142-9384/Printed in the United Kingdom/1010

British Library Cataloguing in Publication Data
Stott, Dave
   50 top tips for managing behaviour
   1. Behavior modification - Handbooks, manuals, etc.
   2. Classroom management - Handbooks, manuals, etc.
   I. Title II. Fifty top tips for managing behaviour
   371.1'024

ISBN 978 0 86388 678 2

Contents

Introduction

50 Top Tips for Managing Behaviour is a practical resource giving many best practice examples for teachers to incorporate into their everyday life at school. Containing pages of proven and successful strategies to use within the teaching and learning environment, it takes a two-pronged approach: firstly, it offers expert advice on how to manage both individual and groups of students; secondly, it backs this up with key reminders to help teachers manage their own behaviour. Not only does this straightforward guidance address issues within the classroom, but the approach is extended across the whole school environment.

Many of the tips and strategies within this handbook are intrinsically linked and are designed to help both teachers and all adults working with children to build skill upon skill. The book takes a holistic approach to managing behaviour and, in order to gain the maximum benefit from the advice offered, users are encouraged to see it as a whole 'menu', of which the individual tips are just a part.

Teachers will find this practical handbook helpful as a training aid or as a very readable 'toolbox' that can be dipped into as the need arises. It is made up of 50 short, 'bite-sized' chapters (or 'Tips') that show the user how to develop a calm, emotionally literate classroom by successfully managing the specific behavioural challenges that face teachers every working day. The book may be read as a whole resource, giving teachers an opportunity to reflect on, question, confirm and evaluate their own practice, but it has also been designed so that teachers who have identified a specific behavioural difficulty can quickly locate detailed and helpful advice.

50 Top Tips encourages teachers to incorporate a range of techniques into their normal management style and to create an on-task environment in which students can learn and teachers can teach. The approach taken within this resource is to encourage teachers to recognise the thoughts and feelings that drive behaviour, and to become more proactive in their management of both chronic and acute behavioural difficulties.

Without the daily disruption of challenging and off-task behaviour, teachers' stress levels can be reduced. This will lead to more positive interactions and thus raise the achievement of all students. The material offered has been drawn from the author's vast experience of observing and working within happy, motivated classrooms and seeing just what makes the student, teacher, other staff and, indeed, the whole school successful.

Author's note

Much of this work was inspired by the Department for Children, Schools and Families' Social and Emotional Aspects of Learning (SEAL) materials, which were issued in 2007. These are curriculum resources designed to help develop children's social, emotional and behavioural skills; one is aimed at primary and the other at secondary schools. Further information can be obtained from www.standards.dcsf.gov.uk/nationalstrategies

Acknowledgements

I would like to thank and recognise the expertise of the many colleagues I have worked with over the years, especially from Michael Drayton School, Nuneaton and Robert Bruce School, Bedford. I would also like to acknowledge the skill and expertise of those colleagues from the multi-professional teams with whom I have had the pleasure of working in Northamptonshire. My current role as a trainer and consultant leaves me in the privileged position of observing the many excellent professionals who work in mainstream and special schools all over the UK. You have all been an inspiration.

Behaviour management during cover lessons

There is a 'double edge' to the problems that arise when providing staff cover for absent colleagues. Firstly, there is the possible feeling of some anxiety when teachers realise that they are not well enough to be at work, or any other reason that compels them to be absent. Most teachers are aware that their absence will cause timetabling difficulties and that their place will have to be covered by a colleague or, in some cases, by supply staff. However, any member of staff forced by circumstances to be absent will feel supported if they have confidence in the systems that are in place to cover such eventualities.

Secondly, feelings of anxiety can arise from the practical difficulties that the loss of non-contact time can generate when teachers are absent from school. Some primary school teachers do not yet have non-contact time built into their weekly schedules. Nevertheless, staff absences still cause disruption to the timetable and will, even in primary schools, mean that some staff are obliged to alter their normal (and prepared) workload. Under these circumstances, it is all too easy for the

behaviour of both staff and students to be adversely affected when their regular teacher is absent. There are many management issues here that should be addressed before such a situation arises. In this way, the causes of stress related to cover can be anticipated and alleviated for all those involved. Consider these stress points:

- Absent teachers, in addition to the anxiety caused by their illness, may be experiencing feelings of guilt about the problems their absence may be causing.

- Staff members in charge of arranging cover may be experiencing feelings of frustration and trepidation, especially when they are delivering the bad news about the absence.

- Teachers having to provide cover may be feeling angry, picked on or under pressure as their planned timetable is unexpectedly disrupted.

- Students in the class being covered may be missing their regular teacher or worrying about how the rest of the class will respond, and, because of their anxiety, may resort to disruptive behaviour.

P This page may be photocopied for instructional use only. © Dave Stott (text) and Bill Stott (illustrations).

To manage these situations, use this three-step approach: plan, prepare and then have a consistent way of presenting the cover lesson.

Step 1: Planning

- Teachers should adhere to an agreed system of contacting the school as soon as they know that they will be absent.
- One staff member should be the nominated person to take charge of cover arrangements (with a deputy available should that person themselves be absent).
- A no-blame environment should be created that promotes a consistent and collective sense of responsibility within the whole staff group.
- A school-wide approach to behaviour management should be established, which allows a consistent response from all staff, but also allows a degree of individuality.

Step 2: Preparation

- The class teacher's behaviour rules, rewards and consequences should be well rehearsed and on display in the classroom.
- A seating plan helps to manage behaviour and is supportive to supply teachers who may otherwise struggle with names.
- Lesson plans, resource lists and procedures should be available in the classroom, and not just in the class teacher's notebook.
- Good practice demands that the teaching environment is kept tidy and well prepared. A well-organised room is of great help for any teacher unexpectedly taking over another's classroom.
- Teachers should spend a moment reflecting on generic approaches to behaviour management before they begin the cover lesson; they should also try to familiarise themselves with the school's expectations and rules.
- A cover lesson is no different from any other lesson and should never be approached empty-handed. Teachers should ensure that they know where spare pens, pencils, paper and other resources are stored. They should carry a collection of additional activities for those students who finish early or have credible excuses for not undertaking the set work. Teachers who 'fumble about' lose respect very quickly.

Step 3: Presentation

The manner in which a cover teacher delivers a lesson should have a positive effect on both the teacher's and the students' behaviour:

- Cover teachers should be clear about their expectations. They need to think about this before going into the classroom, so that they can then command respect by asserting control immediately in a calm and consistent manner.
- By presenting the lesson in a confident way, they will dissuade those students who like to see how far they can bend the rules or push a new teacher.

A staff enrichment programme will help reduce teacher absences by reducing stress. All schools should also have a period of non-contact time and this can generally be managed within the curriculum by bringing in extra resources for perhaps two hours a week. During this period, some time should be set aside for all staff to discuss absences and cover, and then to establish a positive programme, as outlined above. Teachers will not feel resentful about giving up their daily routine, marking or preparation time in order to provide cover if an agreed school-wide policy is in place. It follows that if teachers are not resentful or stressed, class behaviour will be improved and students easier to manage.

Top Tip 1

Establish simple procedures

P This page may be photocopied for instructional use only. © Dave Stott (text) and Bill Stott (illustrations).

Behaviour planning

Few teachers or teaching assistants would take a class, or even a small group of students, without a lesson plan. This is certainly true when a lesson is due to be observed by a senior manager, colleague or schools inspector. Lesson plans will inevitably vary in content and detail, taking into account the subject matter, the needs of the individual students, the resources required and the learning objectives. The curriculum content is generally clearly stated, and the need to have materials at different levels so that all students can access that curriculum is generally understood.

Generic rules and boundaries governing behaviour and applicable throughout the school will be in place, together with some specifically related to a particular teacher or classroom, but these will not necessarily be sufficient to cope with the individual needs of some students. Therefore, in order to successfully manage the behaviour of students within the classroom, which in turn will also be variable, a comprehensively planned approach is necessary. It is vital to include a 'behaviour plan' within the overall plan before commencing a lesson. This level of preparation, together with the ability to employ a range of strategies, is the key to the successful management of behaviour.

Consider how much preparation is usually put into other everyday life situations. For example, anyone who has ever returned an item to a retailer because it was the wrong size, wrong colour or purchased in error will identify with the amount of forethought needed to ensure a positive result:

1 Find the receipt.
2 Replace the item in the original wrapping.
3 Rehearse the reasons for returning the item.
4 Find the right person to speak to.
5 Think about how to be assertive but polite.
6 Identify the required result (a refund, replacement or credit).
7 Prepare a range of responses according to the attitude of the retailer.
8 Be persistent and consistent.

Teachers who are faced with the prospect of working with class groups where behaviour is a significant problem should consider this level of preparation.

Plan for groups and individuals

Assuming there is a lesson plan in place, try adding a behaviour plan. Become familiar and comfortable with the school's behaviour policy. Prepare a transparent set of rules and expectations of behaviour when students are working in the classroom. It is vital that these expectations have been taught and are regularly referred to and reinforced. It is of little use for teachers to have a rule that states 'Follow instructions first time given' when they are prepared to give the same instruction over and over again to students who simply ignore them. This not only causes a dramatic increase in the teacher's stress levels, but also teaches students that rules need not be followed. No teacher wants to feel that the student believes that what is said is not meant.

Every planned approach should include a firm adherence to agreed rules, backed up by a graded, hierarchical system of rewards and consequences. It makes each step clear to the teacher, and students will quickly understand the choices available to them. This planned approach should also include a thorough knowledge of the individual needs of each student in the group. For those identified as having difficulty in managing their own behaviour, an Individual Education Plan (IEP) should always be in place.

Identify each student with an IEP and adhere to the arrangements and targets within it. All adults teaching the student should be familiar with the IEP. It is not sufficient simply to be aware of the IEP; this approach will be effective only if the plan is studied, understood and followed. This familiarity will also enable the teacher to make an informed contribution to the review process for the student's IEP by having clear evidence of the progress made towards achieving the targets set within it. Failure to follow the guidance and arrangements suggested will make it very difficult to measure progress.

 This page may be photocopied for instructional use only. © Dave Stott (text) and Bill Stott (illustrations).

Remain in control

Although targets are an important section of the IEP, it is the arrangements and strategic guidance that contribute to the planned approach. Bearing in mind the 'returning items to the retailer' scenario above, teachers should consider the following when planning to manage difficult behaviour:

- practising self-calming techniques
- revising the student's IEP, noting specific considerations (for example, not invading personal space, using the student's first name, keeping voice volume low, making pre-agreed non-verbal signals to remind the student of the expected behaviour)
- not saying anything that they do not mean or are not prepared to carry out.

The 'planned approach' style will improve consistency and allow teachers to think clearly when confronted with difficult situations. Above all, every teacher's intention should be to remain in control, prevent any escalation of adverse situations, and allow both teacher and student to retain self-esteem.

Top Tip 2

Be prepared!

 This page may be photocopied for instructional use only. © Dave Stott (text) and Bill Stott (illustrations).

Body language

Most teachers have studied the practical ideas given in print or in seminars on behaviour management, which are usually centred on specific strategies and techniques. These sources rarely refer to the teacher's body language. However, by understanding the importance of body language, the 'bigger picture' of the relationship between student and teacher can be completed, and this will be of great help to both.

Thoughts, emotions and feelings drive not only verbal language but also body language, which in turn becomes the visible behaviour that students can see. Non-verbal language is as tremendously powerful as a means of communication as verbal language. This is equally true of students as well as teachers – and indeed of everyone involved in the teaching/learning process. It is quite possible to say one thing when the body language is saying something entirely different. In the case of teachers, for example, rather than conveying the intended message, their body language might lead students (or colleagues) to think that:

- the person doesn't mean what they are saying
- the person is overreacting to the situation
- the person is experiencing high levels of stress
- the person is in danger of 'burn out'
- the person's attempts at self-control are affecting the sincerity of what is being said.

Given this common scenario, to become successful at managing behaviour teachers must look at the 'bigger picture' of what is being conveyed when being faced with challenging behaviour. Thoughts have a direct effect on feelings, actions and, ultimately, body language. In turn, the body language conveyed has a direct effect on the response received. Teachers should imagine watching and listening to themselves in real time whilst the action is taking place. If they have ever actually experienced this often unnerving moment, they will quickly understand how influential body language is.

Our voices do not sound the same to others as they do to ourselves. Most people have experience of listening to themselves on tape and a common response is 'Do I really sound like that?' Everyone has also seen a reflected image of themselves – in a shop window, for instance – and then perhaps altered their stance or posture because they did not like what they saw. In this way, teachers should think about how they might be heard and seen by others – in particular by students with challenging behaviours – because this can have an influence on their ability to manage situations.

Most people are at least subconsciously aware of the impact of this bigger picture. Comments made to students (or even to the teacher's own children at home), such as 'Just look at yourself', 'You're not thinking this through' and 'You don't really mean that', clearly indicate that visible behaviour does not always reflect what is actually happening. It can also indicate that people's actions are not in tune with what they are thinking.

This is also true of the teacher. For example, in a situation where the teacher's real thoughts are saying 'I'm not happy, this student is getting on my nerves', but where

P This page may be photocopied for instructional use only. © Dave Stott (text) and Bill Stott (illustrations).

the teacher is actually saying something entirely different, the student will pick this up from the body language conveyed and react accordingly. Understanding the impact of body language means being in tune with, and able to react to, all the physical and emotional pressures affecting the teacher's ability to manage a given situation successfully. The four main components of this bigger picture are:

1   thoughts
2   feelings
3   body language
4   actions, including verbal language.

In a situation where the student is really getting on a teacher's nerves, the teacher's reaction to the student could range between anger, irritation, sadness, fear or worry. All of these will affect body language. A facial expression that is frowning or staring may indicate fear; a clenching and unclenching of fists may show repressed anger, and so on.

The difficulties teachers face in these situations result when their emotions and body language seem to be out of tune with what they are actually saying. It may be possible, with a lot of self-control, to cope with some situations for a short time, but unless all aspects of the bigger picture are taken on board, it is easy for teachers to revert to typical styles of response. These may be either passive or hostile depending on the individual, but may well be entirely inappropriate, leading to a failure to manage the particular event.

Teachers will therefore benefit not only from being aware of their own 'bigger picture'– that is, how they appear to others – but also if they teach this approach to their students. This cannot be done by talking about the technique alone. They need to find time to role-play situations to enable students (and adults) to actually feel how powerful understanding body language can be in managing their own behaviour and successfully managing potentially explosive situations.

Teachers also need to remember to set clear boundaries for role-play sessions, allowing all participants to practise the skills in a safe and controlled environment. Such practice will enable all concerned to be much more confident and successful when they find themselves in real-life situations.

Top Tip 3
Mean what you say!

 This page may be photocopied for instructional use only. © Dave Stott (text) and Bill Stott (illustrations).

50 Top Tips
for Managing Behaviour

Building positive relationships with 'difficult' students

No matter how tolerant, easy-going and organised teachers are, there will always be students whom they find challenging or 'difficult'. It is not possible to give an exact description of a 'difficult' student. For some teaching staff, it may be the student who is forever causing low-level disruptions such as fidgeting, time wasting, finger clicking or just generally being 'awkward'. In other cases, 'difficult' behaviour may be seen as far more challenging: the student may be argumentative, confrontational or simply refuse to comply with any request. Such students can push even the most tolerant of adults to their limit.

There is also the *perception* of the difficult student to consider. A challenging and argumentative student in, say, the French lesson, may well be a paragon in another class. Many teachers have walked into the staffroom complaining about the problems they have encountered with a particular student, only to be told: 'Well, I never have any problems with him!'

Situations like this are far from helpful in both the short and long term; they can make teachers question, not just their relationships with students, but also their own professionalism and abilities. Indeed, this type of comment may even lead to a loss of self-esteem on the part of the teacher, with a consequent effect on their teaching style.

A definition of a 'difficult' student could be: 'The difficult student is the one whose absence from school makes me happy!' However, simply longing for the student to go away from school, or be moved to a different group, is not going to help the teacher build positive relationships. The problem may seem to have gone away when the student is moved, but it may well reappear with another student. The teacher must be prepared to face change in order to avoid experiencing further difficulties in the classroom.

Building positive relationships with difficult students carries many benefits:

- The student learns from their teacher about building relationships and understanding the importance of empathy.
- Both student and teacher experience short-term (each lesson) and long-term (whole academic year) benefits to the learning/teaching programme.
- When other students and staff observe the relationship they see a real example of role modelling.
- There is less need to use 'behaviour management' techniques and strategies.
- The student and, as a consequence, the classroom remain calmer.

A positive attitude will give the student far greater opportunity to experience success in their lessons, thus improving their level of achievement and self-esteem and, ultimately, their behaviour.

Communicate

It is important to keep in mind the reasons for building positive relationships, and this is true for all students, not just for those who are perceived to be 'difficult'. Teachers should at all times be aiming to provide an environment that allows all involved to achieve their maximum potential. Teachers should be able to teach in a calm environment, and students should have the opportunity to learn without being disrupted by a minority.

When planning how to approach the difficult student, the following might be taken into account:

- What exactly are the issues that cause concern? Identify the specific behaviours.
- When do these behaviours occur? All the time? When the student is asked to 'put pen to paper'? At the start of each lesson? When the student is sitting with certain classmates?
- What have your responses been to date? Are some more successful than others?
- Talk over the problems with another member of staff, listen to their techniques and try to observe the student in other situations.
- Raise the issues with all appropriate parties concerned: student, parent, form tutor, head of year, and so on.

 This page may be photocopied for instructional use only. © Dave Stott (text) and Bill Stott (illustrations).

Once a clearer picture of the student emerges, some light may be thrown on the reasons for their behaviour, and why this particular student is deemed to be so 'difficult'.

The next steps may well take some time to implement. The student may now feel that the school or teacher is 'on their case'. Teachers should remember that they are the role models, and should not be led down the dead-end road of confrontation and reluctance to communicate. This will only prolong the situation. It is therefore worthwhile preparing a range of strategies. This is no different from any other problem-solving process. Once the problem has been identified, think of a range of solutions that should be considered and tried. Some examples are:

- Meet on a one-to-one basis with the student. This should be quite formal and away from an audience. State the relevant issues and try to come up with some solutions.

- Make time to see the student in other situations, such as at change of lessons, in the dining room or at break time.

- Practise some self-calming techniques.

- Be supportive and look for opportunities to use praise. (This can sometimes be quite difficult, but it is helpful for teachers to see themselves as role models in these situations and leave emotions aside.)

- Establish some rapport by, for example, finding a shared interest in a topic, such as a particular soccer club or rock band.

Communication is vital. If the teacher is prepared only to 'deal' with the student during lesson time, the student will – at least in their teacher's eyes – remain difficult and all will be lost.

Top Tip 4

Communicate!
Communicate!
Communicate!

P This page may be photocopied for instructional use only. © Dave Stott (text) and Bill Stott (illustrations).

Bullying

Some form of bullying occurs in most schools, at varying levels and at different times. These behaviours often begin with very young children and can, if no intervention takes place, become entrenched. Excellent ideas such as an 'Anti-bullying Week' can make a difference in reducing the numbers of bullying incidents, but staff must be prepared and able to respond in both proactive and reactive terms. This means schools must develop a whole school framework and ethos within which a social and emotionally aware community may work together in some measure of harmony. Staff will also need skills to respond to incidents that are both perceived and recognised as bullying.

It is vital at the reactive stage that both students and staff are able to identify acts of bullying, which may otherwise be confused with teasing, confrontation or general play. The primary school Social and Emotional Aspects of Learning (SEAL) materials identify the characteristics of bullying as:

- ongoing (this is not the same as conflict between two equals or random unprovoked aggressive acts)

- deliberate

- unequal: bullying involves a power imbalance (this can result from size, number or higher status, or from having access to limited resources).

When attempting to identify forms of bullying, staff may often categorise the worst form of bullying as being that which involves physical hurt or pain. However, the many and varied forms of bullying that take place can be assessed only in the careful monitoring

of the effect the bullying has on the person experiencing it. For some people, a 'look', a carefully chosen word or act, or even a text or email, can be as devastating as any other form of bullying.

When discussing issues relating to bullying it is helpful for staff to be aware of their own and their students' vocabulary. Use terms such as 'the person who is being bullied' rather than 'the victim', and 'the person who is doing the bullying' or 'the person who is using bullying behaviours' rather than 'the bully'. It is important to describe behaviours rather than labelling individuals, which can lead to a resistance to change and thus to permanence. Schools, and staff as a whole, should work hard to ensure that key messages relating to the school ethos are given clearly and regularly to all members of the school community. Measures should also be in place to ensure that these key messages are not only communicated to, but also acted on consistently by, all staff.

In order to create a school environment that is safe and bully free there is a need to understand why children who are bullied and the witnesses of these acts feel unable to report the incidents. Bullying can take many forms. It is very easy for staff to be judgemental about it. The seriousness of the bullying is assessed by giving some consideration to how it made the person who experienced the events feel.

P This page may be photocopied for instructional use only. © Dave Stott (text) and Bill Stott (illustrations).

Bullying will create strong feelings, thoughts and behaviours in all parties. Students, of all ages, need response strategies, a plan and clear problem-solving techniques to enable them to deal with these emotions and behaviours. Teach problem-solving techniques and self-calming strategies to students who are actively or passively involved in bullying. Demonstrate these techniques and act as a role model so that they become a natural and first response when students are faced with acts of bullying:

- Identify the exact problem.
- Think of at least four possible responses to the problem.
- Test these responses with the following questions:
  - Will it work?
  - Is it fair?
  - How would it feel?
  - Is it safe?
- Try the chosen solution.
- Monitor and evaluate the solution.
- If it does not work, repeat the problem-solving strategy.

A whole school approach

It is worth considering where and when the bullying might be taking place. Are there 'hot spots' in the school? Remember that incidents of bullying can occur in the classroom as well as outside. In fact, it is sometimes the adult's behaviour that can be perceived as bullying. Repeated sarcastic remarks about work or behaviour are equally damaging to the student towards whom the comments are directed, and to those who hear those comments.

The teacher's reactions to minor levels of unkind behaviour can be highly influential in stopping this behaviour developing into something far more serious. Teachers must create an environment that values individuals. The school culture should provide opportunities and create an ethos that allows and encourages staff and students alike to talk about their fears and feelings. It is important not only to be able to talk, but to be listened to and understood. Within every school there is a joint responsibility to ensure that similarities and differences are valued and celebrated in an atmosphere of empathy and respect. This can only work as part of a whole school approach.

Following the theme of the whole school approach, it is worth putting up small and easily read posters around the school that highlight respect, care and consideration towards fellow students and staff. So that these do not become stale and therefore ignored, change them frequently. Make sure that the wording is relevant to the school population, and perhaps feature cartoons or other devices to maintain interest.

Top Tip 5

Create a culture of respect

℗ This page may be photocopied for instructional use only. © Dave Stott (text) and Bill Stott (illustrations).

Chronic misbehaviour

What is actually meant by 'chronic' misbehaviour? For many teachers managing what they perceive as 'chronic' misbehaviour in the school environment, the meaning may well be only too apparent. But is 'chronic' misbehaviour different from 'acute' misbehaviour? A definition of the term 'chronic' would include phrases such as:

- persisting for a long time
- constantly recurring
- having a particularly bad habit
- difficult to eradicate.

However, to avoid any confusion with what might be described as 'acute' misbehaviour, the definition of 'acute' is quite different:

- bad, difficult or unwelcome
- short in duration but generally severe.

Although many teachers do in fact suffer with 'one-off' acute behaviour problems from individual students, the concern here is with practical tips for managing the student, or groups of students, who regularly or chronically display unacceptable behaviour in the learning environment.

Major outbursts can be very upsetting, but in most teachers' experiences these occur less frequently than the daily 'drip drip' of relatively minor disruptions. However, it is the cumulative effect of the daily disruptions that causes most damage to the learning process of the entire class group. Teachers become worn down by the problems created by a daily round of minor incidents. Such incidents impair teaching and learning and are often the springboard for more acute and serious behavioural difficulties.

Patterns of behaviour are determined by two main principles:

1 clarity in communicating what is acceptable to students, their parents and the whole school staff
2 creating conditions in which students are actively taught positive behaviour strategies throughout their school careers, within a classroom context designed for quality teaching and learning.

In spite of all the best plans and positive approaches there will always be individual students who cause continuing stress and concern because of their chronic misbehaviour. Experienced teachers have favourite strategies for managing chronic misbehaviour. The following tips may well confirm some of these, as well as introducing new ones to teachers' toolboxes.

Everyday tactics, such as those suggested below, will assist in avoiding the triggers that can cause difficult behaviour:

- moving in close to individuals
- using a low voice or whispered directions/reminders to the target student
- using eye contact to signal awareness of what is going on
- moving the student to another seat, perhaps closer to the teacher
- a change of activity
- stopping the whole group and making a general statement about behaviour
- acknowledging good behaviour
- adopting positive body language.

Meet with the student

For the student who misbehaves every day in spite of the teacher's best efforts, consideration must be given to extending the mode of intervention. At this point the student's involvement is critical to the success of any such intervention. With the cooperation of the student, the first step must be to identify clearly the problem behaviour.

At this stage be very specific. Do not, for example, think of the behaviour as: 'He gets on my nerves, constantly disrupting and annoying everyone around him.' Rather, be positive: 'He is turning round chatting to those around him and when I attempt to get him back on task he constantly answers back.' Alternatively: 'He is constantly tapping on the desk and shouting out across the room.'

Once the problem has been clearly identified, it is time to meet the student on a one-to-one basis. The meeting should be held on the teacher's terms, with the other students unable to hear or see what is happening. The agenda should be pre-planned and the delivery style calm, firm and focused. Try this procedure:

1 State the nature of the problem: 'John, I can't allow you to constantly distract the class with your chatting,' or 'John, your answering back is simply not acceptable.'
2 The student will often reply to the teacher's points with a denial. Make sure that in planning for the meeting, up-to-date records of the student's behaviour are accessible.

P This page may be photocopied for instructional use only. © Dave Stott (text) and Bill Stott (illustrations).

3 Once the point is made it is time to work jointly with the student to arrive at a possible solution to the problem.

4 Agree how the student will be reminded about the behaviour; suggest a strategy such as a target sheet, verbal reminder or private signal.

5 Agree the appropriate behaviour the student should display from this point forward.

6 Agree acceptable rewards and sanctions that will be used when the student chooses to follow or not follow the agreed patterns of behaviour.

7 An important aspect of this type of agreement is the inevitability of the consequences. It is important to be consistent in applying the agreement.

8 Monitor progress and always agree dates/times for review meetings.

Teachers should not expect immediate changes in behaviour and should also be aware that there may be 'blips' even when things appear to be going well. It will have taken some students a long time to establish patterns of poor behaviour. Likewise, it will take some time for them to start making better choices.

TopTip6

Agree a strategy with the student

 This page may be photocopied for instructional use only. © Dave Stott (text) and Bill Stott (illustrations).

Concentration

How do teachers maintain and extend levels of concentration? Do they make the assumption that the student in question is concentrating in the first place? To encourage concentration, differentiated and age-appropriate work is vital, together with teacher delivery, pace and knowledge of the subject. An understanding of learning styles will enable teachers to vary the delivery methods and thus promote inclusion. In every teaching environment there is still a need to have available a variety of strategies and arrangements. Routines, visual and verbal reminders, proximity and voice modelling will all contribute to maintaining levels of concentration.

Frequent failure amongst students to complete set activities or tasks can lead to low-level (sometimes high-level) disruption and is often indicative of poor concentration. This can result in teacher frustration and lack of achievement by the students concerned.

Concentration levels can vary. This is true for everyone: students and teachers alike. Always allow students a certain amount of 'take-up' time – nobody is 'on the ball' for every minute of every session. Many teachers are surprised by the student who is apparently taking no notice of what is happening in the classroom and yet, when questioned, knows exactly what is going on. In contrast, other students who appear to be concentrating may require a little longer to process information and offer a response. Outward or visual signs can be misleading.

When attempting to improve concentration skills, it is very tempting to expect the student alone to make all the changes. Individual Education Plan targets and arrangements are often designed to focus purely on the behaviour of the student, for example: 'To remain seated

for five minutes during a 20-minute period' or 'To be able to answer three questions in context from a teacher-led discussion'. These are fine expectations, but the missing link is how the teacher is going to enable the student to be successful. What are the factors within the learning environment that will give the student the greatest chance of success? The following points are helpful in this process:

- Environmental. Some aspects of the environment are within the control of the teacher, others may not be. Heating, lighting and space are all important considerations. Can the heating in the room be adjusted? Do the windows open? Are all the lights functioning properly? Do the students have sufficient space to sit comfortably? Are they able to store their coats or property? Can they move easily around the room? Are the students drinking sufficient water?

- Seating arrangements. Pay particular attention to the classroom seating plan. How are the students grouped? Is the student who struggles to concentrate seated by the door or, even worse, next to the window? Do the students have to move around the classroom to access equipment?

- Noise levels. Set clear boundaries for different working times. Quiet work, discussion and group work should all be clearly understood and reinforced throughout the lesson. Young children will benefit from visual reminders. Red, amber and green cards to indicate acceptable noise levels work well.

- Reward systems. Try to be positive and proactive. Effective systems need to be structured and hierarchical. A simple smile, thumbs up or a word of encouragement will help maintain concentration levels

 This page may be photocopied for instructional use only. © Dave Stott (text) and Bill Stott (illustrations).

for many young students, while others will require greater levels of input. Do not underestimate the power of low-level interventions. Move around the classroom – proximity is a very sound technique. Use a student's name whilst teaching to bring them back on task or to help them maintain their concentration; remember previous comments about take-up time.

• Time reminders. A very successful technique during learning activities is to use clear prompts. Do not expect all students to be at the same stage in any given activity. Prompt and remind them of time during an activity. Do not expect them to stop one thing immediately and change to another. Tell them instead that a particular aspect of the lesson will be drawing to a close within five minutes: for example, 'You've got five more minutes before you should be moving on to the next activity (or task).'

The 'giving answers' technique

Use this powerful strategy to help maintain and develop levels of concentration with younger children. Give the child concerned the answer, or answers, to a variety of questions that will be asked of the class. Prompt and remind the child that these questions are going to be asked. Ask the child to concentrate on listening for the question rather than struggling to work out the answer.

For example, before a story activity with the class seated in a circle, speak individually to the child: 'Today the story is all about the weather, rain, sunshine, wind and snow.' Next, prepare the child with one or two questions that will be asked in the first five minutes of the story. Establish that the child knows the answers, then ensure that the child is listening carefully for the questions in the context of the class group. Finally, make sure that the question is asked at the appropriate time. Use rewards and praise. The number of questions and answers can be extended as concentration levels improve.

Use clear prompts

P This page may be photocopied for instructional use only. © Dave Stott (text) and Bill Stott (illustrations).

Conflict

Conflict appears to be an inevitable part of everyday life. As more and more conflict is seen in the workplace or classroom, the acquisition of specific conflict resolution skills becomes increasingly essential. Without these skills, communication between individuals or groups can easily break down. To avoid this happening, new skills need to be acquired and extended so that peaceful resolution can occur within a no-blame culture, where individuals are encouraged to take responsibility for their own behaviours. The following skills are all vital components of this process:

- listening
- empathy: the ability to see issues from someone else's point of view
- self-calming techniques
- clear and planned patterns of thinking rather than emotional outbursts
- assertiveness
- knowing how to make up.

It is difficult to resolve any conflict if either, or all, individuals involved do not accept responsibility for their own roles in a given situation. So the first step in resolving any conflict is to identify clearly the roles and responsibilities of the individuals involved. Theoretically, this may seem very straightforward, but problems can arise when it is put into practice because of the high levels of emotion that are often involved. A confrontation can have a variety of emotional and physical outcomes whatever the situation. Skilful management will avoid the worst possible consequences.

Think of the conflict as a 'firework' and then use the following three-stage model as an example of what can happen in an angry confrontation between people:

- **Stage 1**: the match represents the trigger for the conflict.
- **Stage 2**: the fuse is the second step in the build-up of conflict. Once the fuse has been lit, people are physically and emotionally prepared for the fight or flight response. The length of fuse will vary between the individuals or groups involved depending on their resolution skills, tiredness, emotional state and the history between them. Once this point has been reached, it is all too easy to move to the next and potentially devastating stage.
- **Stage 3**: the explosion.

Once Stage 2 has been reached and Stage 3 looms closer, it is unlikely that individuals will be able to employ conflict resolution skills. This is the time when people find it difficult to think sensibly or reasonably. Quite often they have gone beyond rationality. Having reached this point it is difficult to see someone else's point of view. People will probably not understand what they are saying or what is being said – if in fact they are even heard. Finally, those involved will find it virtually impossible to consider consequences or outcomes.

To reinforce the point, here are eight factors that always lead to an escalation of conflict:

1. shouting, swearing
2. name calling
3. accusing
4. interrupting
5. not listening
6. talking over someone
7. making unreasonable demands
8. threatening body language.

Conversely, consider these eight factors that can lead to a reduction in any conflict:

1. active listening
2. understanding the other point of view
3. calm voice
4. calm non-verbal body language
5. not invading personal space
6. finding some common ground
7. admitting the mistake
8. saying sorry (and meaning it).

 This page may be photocopied for instructional use only. © Dave Stott (text) and Bill Stott (illustrations).

The initiatives suggested within the Social and Emotional Aspects of Learning (SEAL) materials map out clearly the initial areas to develop with students:

- Recognise feelings, understand the physical and emotional clues.

- Develop specific skills to manage those feelings. Give students plenty of opportunity to suggest, demonstrate and practise their own self-calming techniques. Role model essential skills in appropriate non-verbal and body language communication.

- Provide opportunities to develop empathy within class discussion and one-to-one meetings.

- Motivate students through class discussion and role play, and provide opportunities for them to understand the benefits to themselves and their peers when they become more proficient at the first two points above.

- Develop social skills by asking students to put into practice their newly acquired techniques.

Problem solving

There are many steps that can be taken with students in order to promote good communication. Start off by providing an area where possible conflicts can be discussed in private. Ask students (and adults) to keep a diary of conflicts they have been involved in and how those conflicts were resolved.

Make conflict a topic in the classroom: pose some examples of conflict situations for group discussion. When doing this, employ appropriate discussion rules using a circle time approach with younger students and the concept of a meeting with older groups. Examples of real-life situations can be used, in which the initial conflict

is acted out, together with the possible resolutions. Go on to develop a problem-solving model so that when the students are sufficiently confident it becomes their first course of action. Here is an example:

1 Identify the problem or source of conflict.

2 Take ownership of the problem and see how resolution can be achieved.

3 Rather than escalate the conflict, try to identify at least five possible solutions.

4 Use the five solutions as the basis for discussion. Think about the eight factors for reducing conflict listed above, including self-calming, listening and empathy.

5 Now run with the chosen solution.

6 Be prepared to return to the discussion stage if the chosen solution is not working or is unsatisfactory for either party.

This positive approach will avoid the emotional hijack, fight/flight response or the 'explosion' in the firework analogy above.

Top Tip 8

Develop a problem-solving strategy

 This page may be photocopied for instructional use only. © Dave Stott (text) and Bill Stott (illustrations).

50 Top Tips
for Managing Behaviour

Consequences

Consequences, or 'sanctions' as they are otherwise known, may be familiar to students, but may often have little or no effect. Merely used as a threat but without any associated action only teaches the student that the teacher is as ineffective as the sanctions themselves. The effectiveness lies in the inevitability of their use and, indeed, in the non-confrontational manner in which they are used.

Begin by noting down all the positive rewards and incentives that are currently used in the classroom to motivate students. These should be the rewards used to reflect good or appropriate behaviour and not those used for academic work. The list may look something like this:

- nod, smile or look of approval
- verbal praise
- sticker or merit
- phone call or note home
- privilege time or free choice.

Every teacher will find a few more to add to the list according to their particular circumstances. However, when compared with a list of sanctions used in response to difficult or inappropriate behaviour, it is much shorter. There always appear to be more negatives when dealing with difficult behaviour and the list of consequences in use may contain:

- 'the look'
- verbal reminder or disapproval
- physical proximity
- moving seat
- leaving room
- loss of privilege or merit
- note or phone call home
- detention, after lesson, during break time or after school
- extra work
- on report
- meeting with parents
- fixed-term exclusion
- permanent exclusion.

This list may not be complete but, compared with the list of positives, it can seem that students gain more attention by doing 'wrong' rather than 'right' things. Will their behaviour really change by drawing on such a menu of negative actions? It is unlikely that a behaviour policy that is heavy on the consequences will be successful.

It is true to say that the above scenario is a generalisation: many schools would disagree with the statement that they

are quicker to issue a consequence than they are a reward. If, however, teachers feel that they are working in an environment in which the reward/consequence ratio is unbalanced, they need to evaluate the effectiveness of both the policy and the practice used within their own school setting. Certainly, if students do not value reward or show any inclination to change their behaviour following a sanction, the system is ineffective and should be changed.

Consequences should be something that students do not like, that do not infringe legal, national, county or school guidelines, and that are effective. They may be used on a school-wide or class-only basis and can also be designed and used within Individual Education Plans. Remember that consequences should be the strongest link between behaviour and change.

Balancing sanctions and rewards

Ideally, teachers should have as many sanctions within their armoury as they have rewards. Sanctions should be used systematically within a graded and gradual approach. The first choice should always be the lowest consequence possible to achieve the desired behaviour. The temptation, which should be avoided, is to use a consequence that is 'overkill' for the situation. This does not give the student the opportunity to make good decisions regarding their behaviour. It also greatly reduces the available options. An appropriate sequence of consequences may look like the following:

- 'Level 1. Use 'the look', or a privately understood signal, to remind the student of appropriate behaviour.
- 'Level 2. Move in closer to the student and use a verbal instruction, reminder or warning. This may be repeated a maximum of three times at this stage. Remember to encourage the student to make a good choice about their behaviour, whilst at the same time attempting to keep the consequences at the lowest level possible.

P This page may be photocopied for instructional use only. © Dave Stott (text) and Bill Stott (illustrations).

- 'Level 3. Move the student to a different seat, possibly closer to the teacher.
- 'Level 4. Instruct the student to stay behind at the end of the lesson, during break time or after school, and fill out a consequence sheet ('what I did, what I should have done').
- 'Level 5. Put the student on report.
- 'Level 6. Contact parent, head of year or head teacher.

These levels are simply suggestions. Teachers are recommended to decide, in agreement with all involved, on the stages and consequences relevant to their own unique situation. The primary concern, however, is that the consequences are used consistently and fairly. The students need to realise that any sanction used is as a direct result of their behaviour and not an emotional response dependent on how the teacher is feeling that day or on which student is being 'picked on'.

It is important to repeat that there should be a clear sense of inevitability about the use of consequences. Students are normally fully aware of the choices open to them, and the ensuing reward or consequence is used to reflect a particular choice. Once a clear and effective graded system is in place, this will make the teacher's life easier because there will not be a time when the next step is not known.

Teachers must not make the mistake of using consequences to hurry students through to the final level, thereby excluding them from the room. The task is to use every available teaching and management strategy to maintain the student in the class with the lowest possible level of consequences.

TopTip9

Establish inevitability

 This page may be photocopied for instructional use only. © Dave Stott (text) and Bill Stott (illustrations).

Creating an appropriate environment

Classrooms, as well as corridors, staffrooms and offices, are all part of the learning environment that contribute to the well-being and effectiveness of the school as a whole. For students, staff and visitors alike, their early impressions form the basis of their relationship with the school, and it is therefore vital that these impressions are good. Impressions start from the moment users enter the school gate and see the building and its grounds. The general state of repair, signage, litter and overall appearance can form a good, or a not so good, first impression that can be hard to shift when trying to create a clear understanding of what the school can contribute to its users.

For many schools this is an ongoing and difficult mission. Problems with budgets, the local community, staffing and the existing architecture all need to be addressed and overcome. This is before the building is even entered. Many users of the building might often view these issues as not 'their problem'. Although individuals feel a responsibility for their own office or classrooms, they may not feel the same way about the shared and general areas.

Establishing a sense of communal responsibility for the environment as a whole is one component of working towards an emotionally literate school. All members of staff and students are able to contribute by being good role models and adhering to the expectations of all users of the building and site. It is important to remember that good behaviour can be 'caught' as well as taught.

It may not be a specific element of a job description, but picking up a piece of litter or reporting damage to the appropriate person really does make a difference. Indeed, encouraging students to pick up discarded items will, in turn, discourage them from littering. The school as a whole then benefits. When asked by a member of staff to pick up litter, many students respond: 'Why should I? It

wasn't me who dropped it.' The point to be made is that both the member of staff and the students in question recognise that litter is unpleasant and that, clearly, it should not have been dropped: that it does not really matter who picks it up – it just needs to be done. There are many points to consider when moving away from the outward appearance of a building and looking more closely at the working environment within the classroom. The following conclusions can be drawn when analysing the classroom environment:

- There are some things that can be changed (displays, seating, access to resources).
- There are additional items that need action, but help and/or funding is needed to bring about change (lighting, general repairs, storage).
- Other issues might also be noted, but responsibility for doing something about them needs to be passed to a third party (decor, building alterations, IT facilities, outside noise).

The critical checklist

Classroom environment checks are always easier, and more effective, if they are conducted with the assistance of a colleague. Joint users of a room (a teaching assistant or a job share with another teacher) should carry out the check as a cooperative venture. Two people can expand the checklist by questioning each other's observations. It is also worth taking into account the views of students who use the room. A second, third or fourth pair of eyes will invariably reveal issues that were missed first time around. Any critical checklist of the teaching and learning environment should include:

- Seating plan: including appropriateness of furniture for all users. There is nothing worse than adults trying to perch on chairs designed for Year 1 and 2 children.

 This page may be photocopied for instructional use only. © Dave Stott (text) and Bill Stott (illustrations).

- Accessibility of resources. For example, how far do students have to walk to find books, pencils, paper or other resources? What about the resultant disruption to other students?

- Storage of both students' and adults' personal property. Students will be reluctant to remove coats and outdoor clothing if there is nowhere safe to store them.

- Displays. Once display areas have been created, ensure that they are updated regularly, and contain students' work as well as school and classroom notices. Torn, damaged work or outdated and faded notices, old class rules, and so on, create a bad impression and lessen the impact of the noticeboard.

- Visibility. This is linked to the seating plan. Consideration should be given to glare from windows and appropriate artificial lighting. Flashing fluorescent lights and dud light bulbs do not contribute to a positive work environment. Computer screens are difficult to read if reflecting glare from windows.

- Heating and ventilation. This may require the intervention of a heating engineer. How effective is the heating? Are the heaters easy to adjust? Do the windows open?

- Noise levels. This is a difficult area for an individual teacher to deal with, but carpet and appropriate flooring, screens, and the use of nearby corridors, all affect concentration levels. If there are problems, ensure that they are raised with the head teacher and in staff meetings.

The above is a snapshot of some of the environmental factors that contribute to the efficiency of the teaching and learning environment. Unquestionably, the environment is a major element in producing a sense of well-being for staff and students; this in turn will have a significant effect on the overall attitude and behaviour of all users.

Top Tip 10
Picking up litter is a positive action

P This page may be photocopied for instructional use only. © Dave Stott (text) and Bill Stott (illustrations).

Crowd control

All adults working in schools and with young people have experienced feelings of panic when normally successful behaviour management strategies fail to have any effect. Panic can quickly give rise to a range of different emotions. These can include anger, despair, frustration, hopelessness and self-doubt, leading to a lack of confidence. When this situation arises with an individual the problem can sometimes seem difficult. However, when teachers are faced with a whole class group, the dinner queue or an unruly group waiting for after school transport, the problem is suddenly multiplied.

Professional development courses, teacher training and general management skills may have prepared teachers to deal with the 'challenging student' or the one-off incident, but how prepared are they when two or more students suddenly join in? A class could be made up of three or four well-motivated and well-behaved students, three or four truly difficult individuals and a remainder of, say, 20 students, who could be classified as the 'grey' group. This last group could go either way. Seeing a teacher struggling to manage three or four difficult students effectively may encourage the 'grey' group to join in the 'fun', and the whole class situation could quickly turn into an entirely different challenge. The teacher is then faced with dealing with a larger group of misbehaving students as the situation suddenly escalates. This is usually at the teacher's expense, and any perceived weakness may encourage any remaining students to join in also.

This scenario is not necessarily confined to the classroom. Lunchtime supervisors are charged with managing large groups of children in a non-academic environment, without the constraints of the classroom, and when school rules and norms may not be applied or seen in the same way. Another challenge is the perceived hierarchy of authority that many children have of the various adults in the school organisation, and they may well adjust their behaviour accordingly.

It is important therefore to develop a range of key skills and strategies that can be called upon when faced with problems from groups of students. Equally important is that these same skills and strategies should be practised, evaluated and developed in discussion with all staff members. The school's expectations and boundaries should also be taught regularly to all students and not just referred to when problems arise.

A particularly useful and effective strategy is to devise a consistent method of gaining student attention. Clapping hands and shouting 'Right then!' in a loud and authoritative voice is perhaps not the best solution when managing a large group of students in, for example, the school hall.

Each teacher should devise their own style and teach this to all the students in their care. The chosen method may vary depending on the situation. In the classroom, for example, a clap of the hands and a vocalised 'right folks!' may mean 'no talking, stop what you are doing and look this way'. Out in the playground, a more suitable audio signal may be a whistle, which means exactly the same as the handclap in the classroom.

Once in a challenging situation, it is often tempting to remain rooted to the spot and use only one 'tool' from the available selection, namely voice. Try moving out from behind the desk, or walk across the playground, approach the group in question and use first names to gain attention and eye contact.

P This page may be photocopied for instructional use only. © Dave Stott (text) and Bill Stott (illustrations).

Tip 11

Move in close

Physical proximity, without invading personal space, can be a tremendously powerful tool when communicating with individual students. In general, when a person is outside another's personal (or social) space – defined as more than 1.5 metres away from an individual – it is very easy for that person to be ignored. Apparently, the other person's subconscious says that it is someone else who is being addressed. So in the school situation, what the teacher is saying may not be seen as applicable by the student in question even though they are the person at whom the remarks are being directed.

Always use clear sentences when giving instructions. Be specific and say exactly what is meant. Many teachers' natural social skills compel them to use words such as 'Please', but it is far more powerful to end an instruction with 'Thanks'. This denotes an expectation that the individual will comply.

Look at this example: 'John and Steven, will you move away from that group and come over here please?' This approach allows too much room for negotiation. Although the two boys may not reply verbally, it is likely that the answer to the request will be 'No'. Even more challenging is the unasked question this now poses '… and what are you going to do about it?'

A better way to phrase the same direction would be: 'John, Steven, you need to come away from the group and move over there, thanks.' The chances of the two boys complying are vastly increased with this approach, and coupled with the teacher's body language, tone of voice and physical proximity, it gives a clear message to all other onlookers.

Remember:

- be consistent
- use body language, not just your voice
- move in close
- use first names.

It is important for teachers to understand that their actions will be observed by all the other students, and the reaction of those students to what has just happened depends entirely on how the teacher handles the situation in the first instance.

Top Tip 11

Give clear instructions

P This page may be photocopied for instructional use only. © Dave Stott (text) and Bill Stott (illustrations).

Deflect the pressure

Interruptions and constant 'I don't understand …', 'How do you spell …? 'and 'What if …?' questions not only cause distraction to other students, but are also a source of unnecessary pressure for both teacher and non-teaching assistant in the classroom.

Even the clearest of introductions and explanations regarding what is required of students often result in a forest of hands, random calling out or the realisation that many students are simply off task. This can lead to pressure and frustration on the teacher's part and disruptive behaviour by some students. There are classroom management programmes that deal with these issues and they suggest that teacher attention is sought by showing hands, coloured cards and a variety of other techniques, all of which are perfectly acceptable in the classroom. Problems arise, however, when there are simply too many students demanding the teacher's attention with questions ranging from relevant and acceptable, to downright time wasting. Often this attention seeking is caused by a failure to listen in the first place.

Many primary school class teachers have experienced the 'crocodile moment' when they turn round from one student to discover a line of children all demanding attention and curling crocodile-like around the classroom. Likewise, within the secondary classroom, time-wasting tactics (endless questions) and interruptions to the lesson, take the teacher's attention away from more deserving and often more pressing issues. In spite of differentiating the work and making allowances for differing learning styles, the pressure created by students, whose only strategy when they have a problem is to seek the teacher's help, is often enough to cause stress and frustration. This, in turn, can prevent teachers from responding appropriately because their patience is tested to the limit. Under this kind of pressure even the simplest of problems can grow into major issues. This can lead to the classroom behaviour plan being temporarily abandoned.

These issues can be overcome largely by teaching students alternative strategies for them to use. It is important here to provide students with several alternatives to that of always using the teacher as their first port of call when faced with a problem.

Many benefits accrue when students employ practical strategies to solve problems without the teacher always being the first option. Providing alternatives allows students the opportunity to develop more self-reliance and self-confidence, teaches them the ability to take risks (no matter how small), promotes a cooperative and interruption-free learning environment and also improves listening skills. Furthermore, this approach will reduce the pressure on the teacher from always being the sole provider of solutions and explanations. Students will develop the skills necessary to find solutions to their problems and difficulties without constant teacher involvement. These are good life skills that students can take away with them and use in situations outside of the classroom and throughout their future lives.

For self-reliant strategies to have any chance of success, they should be taught, questioned, practised and reviewed regularly. Strategies may be general for all students to use or can be individually tailored for students who regularly have specific difficulties.

The following suggestions are strategies that individual students should try before asking for a teacher's help:

- Find the answer somewhere in the room. Is there relevant information on the white board, display or in an accessible textbook?
- Ask another student. Do students have named 'learning buddies'?
- Ask another adult, such as the teaching assistant, in the classroom.
- Students can ask themselves: 'What did I do last time?'
- Get on with something else for a short time, and return to the problem afresh after a break has been taken.

There are many other possible solutions along these lines. Make a list using some of the students' own suggestions. Then whittle down the available choices to the three or four best ones rather than making endless lists of possibilities that may serve only to confuse. Then once these strategies are established, agree with the class that this is 'the way we do things around here'. Ensuring a shared ownership of the chosen strategies is key.

Make sure the system is understood by all students and reinforced both verbally and non-verbally (and rewarded when used). A permanent display of the techniques on the classroom noticeboard will act as a daily reminder. Make the display more appealing by adding some visual clues.

Once this system is working well, the students will benefit by becoming more self-sufficient and able problem solvers. The teaching staff benefit because the pressure is reduced, allowing more teaching time or time to scan, monitor and evaluate. Overall, both the teaching and the learning environment will become more efficient, interruption free and enjoyable for all.

Involve the students

 This page may be photocopied for instructional use only. © Dave Stott (text) and Bill Stott (illustrations).

Empathy

It is only possible to be sensitive and to understand the perceptions of other people if we have the emotional resources to see the world as the other person sees it.
(Faupel, 2003, p12)

Central to the Social and Emotional Aspects of Learning (SEAL) initiatives in primary and, now, secondary schools, is empathy: the ability to recognise and respond to other people's emotions. It is a mature and subtle skill. Responding to the moods and behaviour of colleagues and students in this way also involves sensitivity and the ability to be able to communicate with them.

Simply being part of a group in a teaching and learning environment is insufficient in itself to enable both teachers and students to understand and develop empathetic skills. Although behavioural skills, empathy included, can be infectious, there is a strong case for the key characteristics to be recognised and systematically taught. Empathy is a learned response. Acquiring the ability to see the world through the eyes of another, recognising the pressures they face and subsequently how their behaviour is affected, in turn allows everyone to understand their own behaviours and responses.

In order to create a positive environment in which empathy skills can be developed by both students and teachers, the key characteristics that need to be identified are:

- Observing and understanding the feelings and emotions of others. This is noted through both verbal and non-verbal behaviour.

- Communicating the understanding gained by showing regard for others' feelings.

- Doing one's best to understand the other person's points of view, even though it is not possible to actually experience them.

- Developing the ability to sense the triggers and early warning signs of another person's emotions.

- Appreciating the differences in people's reactions to the feelings and emotions of others.

- Understanding that each person views the world in an individual manner based on their own background and experience. This unique view is what determines their responses and behaviour.

- Developing the skills necessary to be able to adjust or modify one's own behaviour in response to the observed emotions of another person.

- Demonstrating appropriate behaviour for any given situation by developing the ability to recognise and manage one's own thoughts and emotions.

- Developing sensitivity to others.

Although taken as a whole the list above presents a considerable challenge for all primary and secondary school teachers, it is possible to introduce this empathetic approach within the teaching and learning environment.

(P) This page may be photocopied for instructional use only. © Dave Stott (text) and Bill Stott (illustrations).

50 Top Tips
for Managing Behaviour

The primary and secondary SEAL materials promote the development of being able to recognise and manage emotions, and to motivate oneself to achieve targeted goals. They emphasise not only these personal empathy skills but also the ability to apply them in social and group situations.

At the primary school level these skills may be introduced and developed through the use of:

- role play and drama using situations that promote and stimulate varying emotions
- circle time activities with clear guidelines that feature listening skills, turn taking, and expressing and understanding others' points of view
- teaching situations that emphasise verbal and non-verbal language and interpreting and acting on these cues. This might involve the use of video/DVD, audio recording, puppets and drama. Many valuable resources, such as emotions photo cards, are available through school suppliers.

Further activities can be introduced within secondary schools or with older primary students, and include:

- debates, class discussions and drama activities building on the skills and guidelines developed in the previous circle time sessions
- studying different people and cultures, religions and beliefs: appreciating diversity within the school community, the local area and society as a whole.

Across the curriculum

As children mature and grow they constantly question their own identity. They also constantly evaluate their peers and adults as they interact with them and widen their view of the world. Impacting on this are adolescent hormonal changes, together with the stresses and challenges that all students face as they make the transition from primary to secondary school and then on to further education and employment.

Teachers must be aware of these pressures and teach specific skills, such as conflict resolution, anger management and active listening. Make time in all curriculum areas for discussion, a sharing of views and an understanding of varying moral and cultural differences.

Schools will need to work hard to create opportunities across all aspects of the curriculum to develop empathy skills. Where the work is compartmentalised into just pastoral time or 'tutor time', students will not necessarily understand that these skills are transferable skills. It is vital that all stakeholders are involved in this work. This is where the importance of the whole school ethos comes into play as this will allow both teachers and students to apply their new skills to all situations and in all social environments.

TopTip 13

Make it a whole school project

 This page may be photocopied for instructional use only. © Dave Stott (text) and Bill Stott (illustrations).

Ensuring consistency from staff

Whilst recognising the importance of the individuality of all teaching and school staff, it is nevertheless important that they all 'buy into' the school ethos or, to put it another way, 'sing from the same song sheet'. It is vital that staff deliver the same message so that students know exactly what they have to do in any given situation. This approach is no different from the corporate 'house style' approach where staff are instructed in how they respond to the outside world so that customers have one consistent image of the company.

Everybody is different, but that does not preclude them from adopting the same consistent standards. Teachers have been students too and they will recall how their fellow students' behaviour changed according to who was taking the class. Take a moment to reflect on the changed behaviour when the class was taken by:

- the new teacher
- the head teacher
- the supply teacher
- the favourite teacher.

So what is consistency? Many students would describe consistency as fairness, knowing what to expect, and for adults and students to behave within clear, publicised and agreed protocols. This is a good description, and the guidelines or policies should be organised on three levels:

1. whole school policies (what is expected in the school)
2. in-class or faculty expectations (operating under the 'umbrella' of whole school policies)
3. individual arrangements (agreed with individual students).

A quick glance through a school's Self Evaluation Form or the handbook sent out to all new parents, will confirm that these policies do exist. Behaviour policies, marking systems, induction for new staff and reward systems are usually clearly documented. In practice, they can be interpreted in different ways by different individuals and this is where inconsistency comes in. The key to having a consistent approach is to establish workable lines of communication and a common ethos that goes further than a 'mission statement'. This leads to a situation where all stakeholders are able to make a contribution and the skills and abilities of the individual are recognised, whilst at the same time keeping the common aim in focus.

To achieve a level of consistency there should be guidelines that have been agreed by all staff. This is backed up by a system of peer- and self-evaluation as well as frequent reviews. There are two challenges for the school staff. The first is to identify how to integrate these guidelines and policies into the everyday job of teaching in the classroom. The second is to identify how staff can retain their own individuality and approach without becoming the 'rogue' teacher or teaching assistant who is then labelled by students and parents as 'unfair' or just plain different.

COVER LESSON KIT COMING THROUGH!

P This page may be photocopied for instructional use only. © Dave Stott (text) and Bill Stott (illustrations).

Most schools already have several formal systems in place that contribute to establishing consistency. These include:

- published policies that give clear protocols and guidelines within the school
- a Performance Appraisal and Development Programme (PADP) for all teaching and non-teaching staff
- lesson observations
- opportunities to contribute to the self-evaluation process
- a school development plan
- clear job descriptions.

Every teacher should take time to familiarise themselves with the various school policies. These are not written so that a 'box' can simply be 'ticked' and the policies then placed on a shelf. Teachers should ensure that they use the PADP process to identify their own professional development needs, and link this to any action plans formulated from lesson observations.

Communication

On a less formal basis, consistency can be enhanced dramatically by improving communication. With this in mind, it is useful to take an active role in staff meetings. There should always be an agenda and systems whereby staff members can add items for discussion. The goal is to create a staffroom or staff group where colleagues can air problems without fear of reprisal or alienation and where resolution can be sought.

It is important to apply the whole school model to the classroom and ultimately to the individual. Teachers should establish and reinforce their own expectations of how things happen at the classroom level. In order to do this, it is important to understand what happens in other classrooms across the school. There is no better person to observe this than the teaching or learning support assistant, who will have experience of more than one class. Working as they invariably do with a variety of teaching staff on a regular basis, they gain a unique insight into students' thoughts and emotions. The information they hold, through their experience of seeing at first hand the effects of differing styles of approach and consistency in applying school policies and guidelines, is invaluable. They are a resource that should be used.

Consider timetabling meeting times for teachers and teaching assistants to review the day or individual lessons. Each acts as a 'critical friend' to the other and important issues are referred through lines of communication, ensuring that all staff become aware of them.

Finally, at the level of the individual student, teachers must be aware of the agreed arrangements for students with identified needs. Individual Education Plans and Pastoral Support Plans are there to provide an appropriate learning environment that meets the needs of the individual concerned. Consistency should be applied here regardless of lesson, subject matter or teacher.

Top Tip 14

Become familiar with school policies

 This page may be photocopied for instructional use only. © Dave Stott (text) and Bill Stott (illustrations).

Establishing a whole school ethos

The school environment is complex. Students and adults alike must become familiar with the many boundaries, guidelines and expectations that exist. Establishing a whole school ethos can seem, in theory, to be a relatively straightforward step. In practice, however, establishing a consistent and school-wide ethos is altogether different. Policies need to be written, rules and expectations published and induction of new staff and students planned. Group dynamics, individual needs and entrenched ways of working all impact and alter what, theoretically, may seem solid and clear working practices.

Agreed systems and practices that affect all stakeholders at all levels need to be developed and established. The stakeholders in the whole school community include all the students and every adult. As well as the teaching staff, this includes administrators, parents, carers, cleaners, governors and lunchtime supervisors. It is vital that there is sufficient opportunity not only to empower these stakeholders to play an active role in following the agreed guidelines, but also to provide them with opportunities to develop needs-led arrangements and management strategies within their own unique environment.

The complex school structure should therefore address behaviour management issues on three clear levels:

1   the whole school environment – that is, rules, guidance and expectations that are in place and affect all adults and students, all of the time

2   arrangements and expectations that are in place, under the 'umbrella' of whole school guidance, but can be made more specific and relevant to curriculum areas and classrooms, enabling individual teachers to establish their own ways of working with groups of students, again based on the overall whole school guidance

3   individual programmes, such as Individual Education Plans (IEPs), that take account of the individual needs of students; it is important that individual arrangements also take into account whole school as well as classroom arrangements.

Difficulties can arise when students perceive this model as an opportunity to be divisive, playing members of staff off against one another. For example:

- 'That's not how we do things with Miss J!'
- 'That's not fair, Mr S let's me do that.'
- 'How come John's class are allowed to go out?'

Cohesive, clear and, above all, consistent expectations must be taught, modelled and regularly referred to by staff. This must involve all staff, who should have a thorough knowledge of school policies and the working practices of their colleagues.

These policies include the school behaviour policy. This should state clearly the expectations for behaviour in all areas of the school, together with an agreed system of responses to both acceptable and unacceptable behaviour. There should be consistent recognition and vigilant monitoring of behaviour throughout the whole environment:

- Locate the school behaviour policy and become familiar with the content.
- The induction programme for all new members of staff, new governors and supply teachers should include familiarisation with the policy. Ensure that simplified précis versions for very short-term staff are available.
- It is important that parents have access to policy documents.
- Students should be made aware of the whole school expectations. This would normally be on entry to the school as part of their induction. Teaching staff should also regularly refer to these policies and inform students when agreed changes take place. This will ensure understanding and establish consistency.

Subject teachers and class teachers should have clear and consistent work practices when they deal with behavioural issues in their own areas. These practices should support the whole school guidelines, but also be sympathetic to the needs of the particular teaching and learning environment:

- Students should be made aware of their teacher's expectations; they should understand how those expectations fit into the whole school model. This should not be a 'one-off', which is then forgotten – revisit this area regularly.
- Make certain that classroom arrangements do not conflict with whole school guidelines. For example, if the whole school policy is not to allow MP3 players into the classroom, do not relax these rules at any time or in any room. To do so may make the individual teacher popular or gain some favour, but it will undermine the whole school ethos, thus making it more difficult for colleagues to implement these and other rules.
- Allow individuality in subject areas and classrooms within the guidelines established for the whole school.

P   This page may be photocopied for instructional use only. © Dave Stott (text) and Bill Stott (illustrations).

Tip 15

Working with IEPs

There will always be individual students who will need to be treated differently because of their special needs. This is allowed for within their Individual Education or Behaviour Plan. These plans often cover issues other than academic work, so modifications and adaptations to rules and expectations may have to be made. However, these are usually carefully structured and taught to the student and should be seen as special circumstances rather than as flagrant breaches of the whole school policy.

Putting these unique changes into practice contributes to the consistency and effectiveness of the whole school community because they should have been recognised within the whole school ethos. The following points will help when working with individuals who have IEPs in place:

- Be aware of all students within the school who are subject to an IEP or other plan.
- Become familiar with the content of these plans.
- Where appropriate, contribute to the planning, monitoring and review process of these individual plans.
- Do not alter the plans without thorough consultation.

Top Tip 15

Cohesive
Clear
Consistent

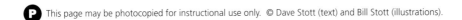 This page may be photocopied for instructional use only. © Dave Stott (text) and Bill Stott (illustrations).

Exclusions

Head teachers and governors are often faced with difficult decisions and real dilemmas when attempting to manage a small minority of students. All students have a right to an education in an environment that is caring, disciplined and orderly. The difficult minority can have a significant negative impact and their lack of education and life chances can result in high long-term costs to society. Education failure affects everyone.

Consider the following typical responses as head teachers are faced with these dilemmas: 'I don't really want to put him out of school for any time. He's been rejected too often already. At home all day or out on the streets will offer him no chance of successful reintegration.' Alternatively, the head teacher may be saying: 'I've had four lots of parents on the phone today threatening to remove their own children if I don't exclude him. I can't let the teaching and learning for the majority of students be dictated to by the behaviour of a minority.'

In an effort to reduce the numbers of exclusions, schools should:

- identify groups or individuals most at risk
- have a range of strategies and expertise available to handle early signs of disaffection
- work closely with all stakeholders, including parents, students, teaching and non-teaching staff and local authority support services.

Exclusion should be used only:

- in response to serious breaches of a school's discipline policy
- once a range of strategies has been tried without success
- if allowing the student to remain in school would seriously harm the education or welfare of that student or others in the school.

Returning a student into the exact situation that has already failed, and expecting them to make all the changes, is unlikely to work. Schools, teachers, parents and students need a range of options that can be tailored, as far as possible, to the needs of the individual situation. A degree of flexibility, innovation and collaboration is also required.

Each situation is unique to the individual and school concerned, so it is not possible to give detailed advice on how to deal with all the variants. However, the following are some practical suggestions to add to a 'toolbox' of responses when setting up a reintegration programme for a student returning to school from fixed-term exclusion:

- establishment of an on-site facility to give the student the opportunity to refocus

- withdrawal from the National Curriculum
- temporary move to another class or set
- dual registration or a managed move to another school within the cluster group.

These are relatively major strategies to undertake and it is more likely that changes to an existing Pastoral Support Plan for the student would be the better (and first) option.

Whenever fixed-term exclusion is used, anxiety and stress levels for the student, parents and staff are always increased. The temptation is to focus on what the student must do or change in order to comply with the requirements of the school or classroom. Although the student may have 'chosen' not to comply with appropriate behaviour, they may in reality be unable to manage themselves successfully. Therefore, expecting them to make all the changes will inevitably be unsuccessful. The first step in successful reintegration is to identify the problem. Do not attempt to do this alone. Gain the views and observations of other staff, parents, students and peers. Once the specific problem has been identified, it is time to come up with a variety of solutions. These should include what can be contributed by teachers and colleagues well as what steps the student can take.

Ⓟ This page may be photocopied for instructional use only. © Dave Stott (text) and Bill Stott (illustrations).

Newly devised or chosen solutions should always be tested:

- Is it safe?
- How might people feel about it?
- Is it fair?
- Will it work?

Choose a solution and use it. Give the solution a time frame and review it. Is it working? If so, great! If not, return to the problem-solving model.

There is often a temptation for teachers (and parents) to feel that they must take on all responsibility for solving the problem. Do not labour under the myth of the good teacher – that is, the teacher who thinks that 'I can solve all the problems for all my students on my own.' That invariably cannot happen. All stakeholders need to work collaboratively and openly, and everyone must be prepared to change their own practice as well as expecting the behaviour of the student to change. Much unacceptable behaviour has taken several years to develop. It is not going to change immediately on return to school.

Top Tip 16

Teamwork is essential

 This page may be photocopied for instructional use only. © Dave Stott (text) and Bill Stott (illustrations).

Flexibility

Flexibility is equally as important as the rules, routines and boundaries that exist in all teaching and learning environments. Every management team, whether in the public sector or in commerce, is encouraged to show some flexibility in how they apply their policies. However, the most difficult of behaviour management skills to master is the ability to make the right judgement about applying flexibility to the overall approach.

All teachers spend valuable classroom time ensuring clarity and consistency with their students, teaching the behavioural expectations for a variety of school and classroom situations. Routines are taught as part of the daily curriculum, regularly practised and always positively reinforced. Most teachers are familiar with the old saying: 'Catch them when they are doing the right thing and then use positive praise.'

It sounds easy in theory, and when used well it is a strategy that certainly does work. However, there will be times when it is all but impossible to find an occasion when an individual student (or sometimes the whole class) is doing the right thing. In these circumstances, the natural temptation is to be negative, raise stress levels and eventually hand out sanctions and consequences. The positive relationship between student and teacher, which may have taken weeks to develop, can quickly dissolve during a lesson that becomes confrontational and intolerant.

There are some occasions – and it is very important to note that these will be few and far between – when teachers may need to be flexible and prepared to make some allowances if they are to maintain their self-control. This may even increase the respect that students already feel for their teacher. Meeting all situations head-on and adhering strictly to the agreed rules in an over-rigid management style allows absolutely no leeway for either teacher or student. There are times when flexibility is a prerequisite for good order and, as a role model, the teacher should be able to recognise these occasions. Quite often, flexible thinking and flexibility in actions will resolve issues rather than allow them to escalate out of control. Recognising this point is perhaps one of the most subtle of all teaching and behaviour management skills to master.

A flexible approach should be clearly and carefully thought through. The flexibility should be in the teacher's thought processes rather than in their normal, everyday practice. Over-flexibility in management style might be misinterpreted simply as weakness and encourage some students to test and push the boundaries. It is important to consider each situation before taking action:

- Will a head-on approach or a refusal to move cause the situation to escalate?

- Is the confrontation or refusal to comply due to issues other than simply defiant behaviour? For example, the last lesson on a Friday afternoon can be challenging, as can the first lesson after a rainy lunchtime, or perhaps the class is restless following a difficult lesson with a colleague.
- Is the teacher tired?
- Is it the end of term, with the Christmas or summer break just around the corner?

Challenging moments

In tricky situations, therefore, it is often best to take a flexible or alternative approach. Individual teachers should determine their own appropriate style of approach or flexibility. What works for one may not be acceptable to another. If the whole class group is restless, tired or simply not in the mood for more academic work – perhaps because it is the end of the week, the day is hot or the half-term break is only a matter of hours away – rather than insisting on total compliance and zero tolerance, it may be time to take an alternative look at the management skills employed.

Situations may arise when teachers would normally expect compliance and strictly observed rules, but realise that this would simply inflame the underlying problem. This is when it is time to negotiate and offer alternatives:

- Give the students regular breaks in their work.
- If the weather is hot and the atmosphere is 'edgy', take a break, go out into the playground or on to the field to complete the lesson.
- Allow a period of time for free talk or chat for your students to let off some steam.
- If the problem is with an individual student, consider backing off and allowing the student some time and space.
- Set shorter, easily achievable targets. Allow the students to work in shorter but concentrated periods of time. Focus on rewards for achievement rather than on sanctions for non-compliance.

On rare and on some special occasions, it is worthwhile settling for less productivity and being more flexible in the regular style of approach on the basis that a smaller amount of work is better than no work at all. Negotiation is easier to accept than zero tolerance. Flexibility is better than confrontation.

Top Tip 17

Quite often less is more

 This page may be photocopied for instructional use only. © Dave Stott (text) and Bill Stott (illustrations).

Gaining attention

Gaining students' attention

The whole class is busy and actively engaged in a variety of learning activities, such as discussion, partner work and quiet reading. The teacher is moving from group to group, dealing with individual difficulties and scanning the class to check on general behaviour. A range of strategies is being used to reward appropriate behaviour and to refocus any off-task students. Sometimes the teacher will want to address the entire group, and sometimes individual students will need to speak to the teacher. It is interesting to note the strategies generally used, compared with those available.

Clapping hands or using a loud voice – directed at no one in particular – with random words or non-words is rarely a successful technique in gaining the attention of a whole group of students. It often results in a need for the teacher to repeat the technique, but louder next time. This can cause confusion for students, a rise in the overall volume and, very often, a sense of frustration for the teacher.

What happens when a student wishes to attract the attention of a teacher? Quite often the student has a problem, a question or an observation – all of which are legitimate reasons for seeking the teacher's attention. The traditional 'hands up' may work well for some teachers, but the problem with this system is that it can leave some students with one hand in the air for several minutes and they become frustrated or annoyed because they have not been acknowledged. Eventually they give up.

Younger children often use the 'hands up' technique, together with shouts of 'Miss, Miss!' or 'Sir, Sir!'. Add to this the common finger-clicking strategy and the once calm, purposeful learning environment becomes noisy and annoying for teacher and children alike. With no clear, taught strategy to attract the teacher's attention, a child may take the next step and get out of their seat. Suddenly, other children also seeking attention are at the front of the classroom crowding the teacher's workspace.

There are numerous strategies, any of which may be successful for the individual teacher, to gain the attention of the whole class or group. Whichever is chosen, the key to success is to take the time to teach the strategy or strategies to the whole class. Be very clear and explicit in explaining how it works. Check for understanding, allow the students to practise the strategy and, finally, review it on a regular basis.

One such strategy is for teachers to clap their hands accompanied by a comment such as 'Thanks, class.' For students to fully understand and comply with this there needs to be careful explanation. For example: 'When I clap my hands and say, "Thanks, class", I want you to stop talking, put everything down and look this way.' Then check with three or four students to make sure that they have understood, by asking them, for example: 'What am I going to do? What do I want you to do?' Ensure that all the points are covered and reinforced.

Then ask for any questions, giving the opportunity for students to raise anything that is not clear. Finally, spend some time practising the strategy, not forgetting to recognise and reward those students who manage to get it right.

Once a chosen strategy has been established, maintain it. Do not be tempted to try something different the following week. This will result in confusion for both teacher and students. It is possible to teach and maintain almost any strategy in this manner. Raising hands, counting down, standing in a particular position in the classroom or ringing a bell are a few attention-gaining strategies that can be successful, but whichever is chosen has to be taught.

Attracting the teacher's attention

The same clarity of teaching must be employed when determining strategies for students to attract the teacher's attention. It is not safe to assume that students will automatically 'know' how their teacher wants them to behave.

Hands up or red/green signs on tables (easily seen when the whole class is being scanned) are perfectly acceptable techniques. At this stage also teach students to have

 This page may be photocopied for instructional use only. © Dave Stott (text) and Bill Stott (illustrations).

'stand-by' activities when it is obvious that their teacher is unable to deal with them immediately. This takes away the chance of boredom, anger or frustration when waiting for a response. Some students will require reminders even when this technique has been practised: 'Ok, John, I'll be with you in a couple of minutes. Do you remember what you could be doing whilst you're waiting?'

Once again, it is important that a consistent way of doing things has been established in the classroom. Routine and consistency can be the key for many students and teachers. Leave the details in an accessible format clearly visible in the classroom. This will reinforce the teacher's methods to the students and remind the teacher about the steps that have been agreed. It will also help the supply teacher, who can come into the classroom and log into the system without delay.

Top Tip 18

Stick to one chosen strategy

 This page may be photocopied for instructional use only. © Dave Stott (text) and Bill Stott (illustrations).

Home–school contact

There are no doubt thousands of unread newsletters and school information sheets lying undisturbed at the back of book bags and the bottom of rucksacks. More often than not, when these notes are found by parents and carers they are several weeks out of date. School staff can often be left wondering why there was such a low turn-out for the last Parent–Teacher Association event or why so many parents did not know about the field trip. And how is it that a student's carers did not know about the problems the school have had with their son? In all these cases, letters will have been sent home with the student. The result is that head teachers and administration staff can spend many hours following up letters and answering telephone calls from parents trying to find out what is happening at the school.

There is a vast array of established ways of communicating between home and school. Homework diaries, newsletters, stickers, postcards, 'well done' notes and the head teacher's letters, which might say: 'Dear Mrs Smith, I am sorry to have to write to you about your son …', are all familiar methods of schools making and maintaining contact with students' parents or carers. Variety is not the problem, however. The key to effective home–school communication is finding the means that works for the school concerned. 'Works', in this context, means not just getting the message beyond the school gates, but for the message to serve its purpose and be acted upon by all concerned.

During the Assertive Discipline (Canter & Canter, 1992) training sessions relating to home and school contact, it was shown that the positive note home was the single most influential method of changing students' behaviour. This has since been recognised and developed, through both published documents from a variety of school publishers, to the innovative and successful systems developed by individual schools themselves. Perhaps the multitude of pieces of paper that parents receive is a problem in itself, however. Parents can feel bombarded with too much information, and some parents are better able to deal with this information than others.

Establishing a policy

Consistency and routine are probably the major issues to get right when setting up home–school links. Students arrive home from school with a variety of pieces of paper that often do not appear to come from the same source. Lessons could be learned here from commercial communications, for which it is emphasised that there must be a consistent way of presenting information.

In addition to consistency in presentation, students as well as parents could be trained to expect letters and forms from the school on a particular day of the week, for example, rather than the random distribution that currently takes place in many establishments. Although most teachers may wish to continue with their own familiar systems, it is important that communication also becomes part of the whole school ethos. The following points should be kept in mind:

- Nominate a member of staff to take responsibility for home–school contacts. This avoids problems such as repetition, confusion and inappropriate contact, and ensures a consistent style of communication.

- Make sure that newsletters are published to a regular schedule.

- Use technology. Set up a school website and encourage parents to log on for current information. Use this in conjunction with printed paper information.

- Standardise all letters, certificates and other printed items to avoid individual teachers producing quirky and perhaps, in extreme circumstances, offensive, materials.

- In agreement with parents, use a variety of modes of communication. Emails, texts, faxes and direct personal contact (home visits) can be powerful and effective. Some parents may use emails all the time, other parents may find printed matter difficult to access because, for example, English may not be their first language.

- Run training sessions in the IT department for parents, to encourage the use of computer technology.

- Ensure that a log is kept of all home–school communication. It is often easier to do this if all letters, certificates, emails, texts and faxes are sent via the school office. This log should also be recorded on individual students' school files. Establish a communications policy and make sure that all staff agree with the reasons why this is necessary.

- Find parents with professional communication skills (journalism, marketing, graphic design, IT, for instance) and ask them to volunteer their skills towards establishing an effective school-wide communication system.

Plenty of planning and preparation needs to go into the smooth running of parent evenings. Sessions that are supposed to adhere to appointment times but overrun, leaving parents frustrated, can do more harm than good in establishing good home–school relationships.

 This page may be photocopied for instructional use only. © Dave Stott (text) and Bill Stott (illustrations).

Finally, do not assume that the teaching staff have all the answers. Provide regular opportunities to seek the opinions of both parents and students on their own ideas about appropriate methods of communication. What may appear to be a good system may not work for some students and parents, and may turn out to be thoroughly annoying for others. Involve all stakeholders and stress the importance for all concerned of an effective communication system. Once one has been found, use it, evaluate it and make changes if necessary.

Top Tip 19

Seek outside help

P This page may be photocopied for instructional use only. © Dave Stott (text) and Bill Stott (illustrations).

Learning techniques from colleagues

Everyone in education recognises that students have differing learning styles. This is also true of adults. Once teachers have qualified, it is entirely possible for them to experience a career during which no further formal training takes place. This is a highly unusual scenario due to the existing systems of performance management and continuing professional development available to all teachers, but nevertheless it is still possible!

All schools have teachers with extensive skills and experience. These teachers are a rich source of learning opportunities for their colleagues. Try conducting a survey within the school and discover the breadth and depth of experience that exists. Training, experience and ability will be both varied and extensive. Schools would benefit if they provided opportunities for these in-house skills to be used, thus making the most of the readily available expertise.

Encouraging skill sharing and cooperation between teaching staff has positive benefits for all concerned, and in particular for students. Responding to a colleague who is having difficulty with a student by saying 'Well, I don't' is not at all helpful. Not only can it dent the complaining teacher's self-confidence considerably, but it also fails to capitalise on the opportunity to skill share. If a teacher does not have trouble with a particular class or student, rather than brag about it and attempt to boost their own self-esteem, they should use the opportunity to share their successful techniques. This kind of cooperation emphasises a school that is working together for the common good, creating a positive atmosphere for staff and students alike.

In order for true skill-sharing activities and in-school support systems to be successful, it is vital for a school to create an emotionally literate environment amongst the staff. Colleagues should feel comfortable about identifying and declaring problems and, in turn, value the skills and expertise of their peers.

Formal and informal skill-sharing and professional development opportunities need to be provided. These opportunities should include meeting the needs of individuals following lesson observations, cascading information to staff groups, and providing the opportunity for skill sharing to take place where members of staff are able to shadow or work alongside colleagues. A particularly successful method of sharing ideas and techniques is to jointly devise subject matter, delivery techniques and Individual Education Plans (IEPs) for students with identified learning or behavioural difficulties.

Use existing opportunities

In most cases existing work practices need not be revised. It is probably more efficient to look at the day-to-day opportunities that already exist and build on those. Try the following:

- Joint planning, either in departments or year groups. Staff should consider not just the content of the curriculum in these planning sessions, but also the mode of presentation, techniques and strategies. With all staff contributing to this process, new strategies, as well as reminders of the old, are refreshed and considered.

- Use existing in-school agreements and time allocated to lesson observation and feedback sessions. These can be organised formally or operated in an informal manner when staff are team teaching. This informal system works particularly well when a teaching assistant and teacher are working closely together. Questions to ask at this point are: Has enough time been allocated to discuss techniques and strategies? Do staff feel comfortable when engaged in this type of activity? Are outcomes of the discussions acted upon? How are the outcomes monitored and evaluated?

- Regular and pre-planned staff meetings for information, strategies, and so on, which are then cascaded to and shared with all staff.

- Ensure that the arrangements section of all IEPs or Pastoral Support Plans are discussed with all relevant teachers and professionals.

- Use some non-contact time to shadow colleagues. Not all colleagues have these opportunities on a regular basis, but where possible take time to observe the styles and strategies of other members of staff. Remember that behaviour can be taught and 'caught'. When shadowing colleagues, focus on specific issues, such as body language, tone of voice and specific behaviour management techniques. Do not just watch the other person, observe in a structured manner and take notes if necessary.

Never take a negative view when observing colleagues. In the classroom it is easy to spot immediately the misbehaving student, whereas the student who complies with expectations tends to melt into the background. This is also true when observing colleagues. Be positive and concentrate on the subtleties because that is where the true work is done. Good and successful practice can be noted and used elsewhere. Remember that the

 This page may be photocopied for instructional use only. © Dave Stott (text) and Bill Stott (illustrations).

Tip 20

purpose of these observations is to discover new ways of dealing with situations. No teacher can manage every situation, and colleagues are the most readily accessible form of professional help available. This is a two-way process and at some stage the roles will be reversed, with the helping teacher seeking advice from another.

Top Tip 20

Build on what is already there

P This page may be photocopied for instructional use only. © Dave Stott (text) and Bill Stott (illustrations).

50 Top Tips
for Managing Behaviour

Low-level techniques

In managing the more challenging behaviours present in classrooms, it is easy to overlook the well-tried and successful low-level techniques. A key element of good practice in behaviour management is the use of prevention. Dealing with potential difficulties before they escalate creates a teaching and learning environment that successfully meets the needs of both teacher and student.

Many years ago teachers were described as people who had '… eyes in the back of their head' – some more so than others. These were the teachers who managed their classrooms with an awareness of all students, often stepping in before a disruption actually occurred. This style of classroom management is not a random system that sometimes works and sometimes ends in chaos. It is a carefully structured and well-practised series of strategies, consistently applied throughout the teaching day.

Successful classroom managers do not focus simply on one activity at a time – that is, taking the register, preparing/handing out work, assisting an individual student – rather, they are 'multi-tasking', using regular verbal reminders, non-verbal signals and visually scanning the whole room. This is a proactive, rather than a reactive, approach to classroom management. The intention is to reduce or eliminate incidents that have the potential to escalate into more challenging situations.

It requires the teacher to be aware of the whole environment, and to structure the classroom in such a way that all areas are accessible. Rather than being confined to the desk or working with specific groups of students at the expense of others, the proactive teacher is highly mobile.

It is worth reflecting on some of the low-level strategies that are often overlooked and even discarded in favour of techniques that are perceived to be more effective. Low-level strategies, delivered in the correct manner and at the right time, can be extremely powerful. The 'right time' is before the problem escalates. Most challenging behaviours have often built up from a low-level start. It therefore follows that to 'catch' them early, and to manage them effectively before they 'get out of hand', will require an equally low-level strategy.

The intention behind using proactive and preventative strategies is to:

- prevent the problem from escalating
- allow the student time and opportunity to choose a more appropriate course of action
- maintain a calm and stress-free teaching and learning environment.

A strategy checklist

The following strategies are neither difficult to use nor 'new' to most teachers' toolboxes of techniques: indeed, you met some of them in Tip 9, 'Consequences'. They are, however, often overlooked.

- **The 'look'**. Eye contact with the target student is often a sufficient reminder to the student to employ more appropriate behaviour.
- **Proximity**. Move into the personal space of the student. It is often unnecessary to speak, as the teacher's presence is likely to have the desired effect. Be aware of the importance of body language when moving in.
- **Scanning**. Constantly scan the room for both appropriate and inappropriate behaviour. It is vital to comment on students who are complying with the guidelines of the classroom as well as those who need reminding.
- **Non-verbal signals**. Encourage students to be aware of meaningful gestures and signs – having to keep voicing instructions can disturb other students. Thumbs up and finger on lips are two simple examples, and there are plenty more that can be devised.
- **Naming**. Use the target student's name during the lesson. Everyone responds to their first name, regardless of the environment. The intention is to gain the eye contact, respect and attention of the student.

 This page may be photocopied for instructional use only. © Dave Stott (text) and Bill Stott (illustrations).

- **Timed reminders**. Once a task has been set, it is important to remind students regularly of progress. Do not expect them to change immediately from one task to another without fair warning. Try a count down: 'You have 10 minutes left for this task', 'Three minutes left, be finishing off now.'

- **Seating**. It is important to have a seating plan in the classroom. Students who are prone to off-task behaviour need to be seated away from distractions, such as windows, outside noise and open doors. Consider who sits next to whom and move students when required.

- **Visual clues**. Use visual reminders for class rules, noise levels and time left. The old-fashioned 'clapometer' type of reminder about noise levels is an excellent practical visual clue. This can be a simple arrow that pivots between red and green in response to the noise level. Highly sophisticated systems are commercially available, but a cardboard arrow pinned to the wall is equally effective.

These are just a few ideas that could be termed low-level strategies. The more they are used, the more the teacher will be able to maintain an equally low level of anxiety, disruption and stress in the classroom.

Top Tip 21

Don't overlook the obvious

 This page may be photocopied for instructional use only. © Dave Stott (text) and Bill Stott (illustrations).

Lunchtime

'It can take the best part of an hour to sort out all the problems and upsets which have happened during the lunch break!' This is a familiar scenario in many schools. Instead of the lunch hour being an enjoyable social occasion, a time when all those social skills learned in the classroom can be put to practical use and extended into the playground, the hour can often be fraught with frustration and arguments. Indeed, the problem is so great in some schools that they have chosen to restrict the length of the lunch break to prevent problems occurring.

Lunchtime is an important opportunity for students to relax and engage socially with one another; equally important is the relationship between teaching staff and the lunchtime duty supervisors. A recent change in title from 'dinner lady' to 'lunchtime supervisor' plays a part in developing a joint understanding and consistency of approach for all the adults working in the school. Consider some of the existing difficulties with which the lunchtime supervisor has to contend, even before the bell rings:

- Many of the children already know them. They are very likely to be the parent of one of the children in the school. Other children may already know a lunchtime supervisor as 'auntie' or they may have a 'friend of the family' relationship with them. This is especially the case in smaller communities.

- Lunchtime supervisors are working with greater numbers of children than single class groups.

- There are no classroom walls in the playground.

- Children may have preconceived ideas about lunchtime supervisors.

- Lunchtime supervisors often have little or no training; they might not even be given an induction into their role.

- Their contractual hours usually coincide with the start and end of the lunch break. This gives little time to prepare at the start of the session or to give feedback at the end.

- They may not be included in staff or school-wide meetings.

Lunchtime can be a time for children to consolidate strong, sometimes lifelong, friendships with one another or to discover a shared interest with their peers. It is a time when they may have the opportunity to confide in or share problems or interests with another adult. The lunchtime supervisor is often the person they can trust, feel safe with and respect. This relationship could be a consistent link outside of the more formal relationships within the classroom. Without doubt, the role of the lunchtime supervisor is demanding and skilful. It is a vitally important role for the individual child as well as for the whole school community.

P This page may be photocopied for instructional use only. © Dave Stott (text) and Bill Stott (illustrations).

A number of issues need to be considered and acted on if the lunch break is to be a positive experience for teacher, child and lunchtime supervisor. Many of these issues may reflect the needs of the individual school and its community. Nevertheless, there are several generic tips that can be applied and which will contribute to the development of the whole school as an emotionally literate environment. Importantly, teachers should get to know all the lunchtime staff and relate to them as equally important members of the same school team. Children quickly pick up on the relationships between all adults in the school. The perceived hierarchy from head teacher down to teaching assistant places lunchtime supervisors near the bottom of the list. If they are seen as 'at the bottom', they will not always be treated with the respect they deserve.

Induction for all new staff

Lunchtime supervisors should be both familiar and comfortable with the school rules. They should be aware of the established system of rewards and sanctions, especially where these are lunchtime specific. These should be communicated to lunchtime supervisors as a normal part of the induction process.

There is often a high turnover of lunchtime staff and consideration should be given to new staff. A thorough induction programme is absolutely vital. No useful purpose is served by sending a new recruit straight into the playground without a formal briefing.

As key members of staff, lunchtime supervisors should have access to all the necessary housekeeping issues. They should know about storage facilities for belongings, they should have copies of behaviour policies and they should have a clear brief on what to do when the weather is wet.

Although all this is subject to management decisions and budget, it is worth considering the contractual conditions under which lunchtime supervisors work. They should be employed for at least 15 minutes before lunch and finish at least 15 minutes after the end of the break. This gives them the opportunity to liaise with classroom staff or share organisational arrangements. Lunchtime supervisors must be included on the relevant parts of in-service training days. They should also be included in the school professional development budget.

When treated as important members of the school team, lunchtime supervisory staff will become:

- confident and able to remain calm
- fair and non-judgemental towards the children
- excellent role models in both verbal and non-verbal behaviour
- proactive and familiar with the school's reward/sanction system
- Important stakeholders in the life of the whole school
- key contributors towards the consistent application of the school's policies.

By including the lunchtime supervisor in this way the school displays clear evidence that all staff routinely include emotional literacy and the development of appropriate behaviour skills beyond the taught curriculum.

Top Tip 22

Treat your lunchtime supervisor as a team member

 This page may be photocopied for instructional use only. © Dave Stott (text) and Bill Stott (illustrations).

Making good behavioural choices

Teachers, classroom assistants and administration staff come into contact with a wide range of young people in their daily routines. Some of the young people they work with have not mastered many of the behavioural skills that staff often assume they should have acquired. Some students have simply never been taught what is and what is not acceptable according to the environment in which they find themselves. In some cases, parents may have been unsupportive of their children and allowed them simply to push the boundaries, or they may have given them no boundaries whatsoever. Some children have been forced to learn by trial and error. Others have not learned at all.

It is possible that a few students may never have had their behavioural problems addressed. Perhaps each of their teachers assumed that the previous teacher or school taught the essential behaviour skills needed in their classroom. No one may have actually taught them skills such as how to enter a room, how to leave a room or how to ask for help, the end result being that the student may invariably make the wrong choice and then has to suffer the consequences of not having been given the necessary tools with which to thrive in the school environment. On the other hand, there are some students who have been taught all the right skills and have a clear understanding of what is expected of them, yet make a conscious choice not to behave or follow the rules.

The teacher's job is to provide an enriched learning environment in which students are encouraged to be motivated, enquiring and independent. In this context, some students are simply exercising their right to choose their own behaviour. Unfortunately, that may mean that they interrupt their own learning as well as that of their peers. It also tests the patience and professional ability of their teachers.

So how can teachers enable students to make good behavioural choices? It is insufficient simply to have the school and classroom rules displayed in the classroom and around the school. Referring to the school handbook and threatening all kinds of sanctions when poor behavioural choices have been made can be futile with some students. These choices are often made for other reasons, such as trying to gain the teacher's attention or the approval of their peers. Attention-seeking students who chronically misbehave often intentionally make poor choices: there are students who enjoy their 'best at being bad' label.

Under these circumstances, the teacher's role is to give the student the tools to help them make appropriate behavioural choices in the first place. In order to do this, teachers need to develop specific skills and strategies. These skills will help motivate their students and enable them to make the types of behavioural choices that begin to move them towards respecting their own (as well as their peers') learning opportunities.

Classroom rules, and indeed the school rules, should be taught to all students from day one, and they should be referred to regularly. Display them in both written and pictorial format in the classroom. Always recognise the student who has followed the rules or guidelines. When rewarding them, be specific and use the opportunity to show how the behaviour that is being rewarded is supportive of the school rules. Explaining why the student has been rewarded helps other students understand the practical application of the rules as well as their importance.

Reinforce the rules

Essential rules, such as fire practice, are reinforced on a regular basis. Students accept the importance of these drills and, indeed, can often get quite excited by them. Bring the same level of expectation into the rest of the rule book so that students begin to understand that the rules are there for very valid reasons and are not simply a list of 'do's' and 'do nots' designed to make their lives a misery. Some adults expect many students to understand and absorb behavioural expectations after being told just once. That does not work: behaviour needs to be taught and reinforced in the same way as any other part of the curriculum. In this regard the following is helpful:

- Be specific in the rules or expectations.
- Tell students exactly what is expected of them.
- Check for understanding.
- Practise the skill.
- Refer to the rule or skill as often as required.
- Use appropriate rewards for good choices.
- Evaluate and change if necessary, remembering that if expectations change, then they need to be taught again.

 This page may be photocopied for instructional use only. © Dave Stott (text) and Bill Stott (illustrations).

There are some students on whom constant teaching and reinforcement of behavioural expectations will have no effect whatsoever. There will always be students who make the choice not to comply. For these students the teacher's own strategies, such as those listed below, are likely to be more effective than general rules and expectations:

- Give clear directions to students.
- Rather than following non-compliance immediately with a sanction, give the difficult student time and physical space in which to decide on their choice of behaviour.
- Do not put them under physical or emotional pressure.

Backing a difficult student into an emotional or physical corner will often result in stubborn non-compliance or, worse still, severe confrontation. The teacher, as the adult, must be prepared to give a little, not to compromise, but in order to help the student make a good choice. Flexibility is sometimes an excellent strategy!

TopTip23

Good behaviour can be taught

 This page may be photocopied for instructional use only. © Dave Stott (text) and Bill Stott (illustrations).

New school year

Schools, teachers and students all have the opportunity to celebrate two fresh starts each year, one in January and the other in September. People return to school in January after the holiday with new resolve and expectations. In September, everything is new – a new class, perhaps a new teacher and new faces within the class. After a long summer of holidaying, socialising and perhaps even boredom, students and teachers alike come back to a new regime with different and renewed expectations.

For the teacher, each new start is an opportunity to remember all those good intentions and approaches that could not be introduced mid-term. Consistency, a planned approach and self-calming techniques are some of the opportunities that now present themselves.

As for the students, September is the time of year when they form lasting views of their new teachers and fellow students. It is a time when all those tried-and-tested methods of pushing the boundaries and making their mark in the classroom or school environment are, once again, put into practice. They will feel their way through and see if their old practices work in this new school year.

What actually happens after that is often determined by the amount, and quality, of preparation that has taken place. For the teacher, the extended break is, quite rightly, a time to rest, recuperate and recharge the batteries ready for the new term. However, it is also important to have spent some time reviewing and evaluating the successes and failures of the previous year. This must include some consideration of behavioural management techniques. Teachers should recall their approach. Was the methodology haphazard? Did students know what to expect from one lesson to another? Was the teacher determined and single-minded? Was the teacher willing to change – to listen to a colleague's suggestions? Now that the Social and Emotional Aspects of Learning (SEAL) initiative has been launched in secondary schools, there is a clear requirement for some teachers and teaching assistants to evaluate their style of working and review the content of many of their lessons. It is important that all teachers familiarise themselves with SEAL.

A teacher's knowledge of the new term's students will help in preparing for the coming year. Take time to look at the class lists ahead of the new term and discuss this intake with the teachers who worked with them previously. This is important, especially when considering the following:

- seating plans
- Individual Education Plans and the arrangements that may have to be made to accommodate any requirements that arise
- the class behaviour plan
- classroom rules

- rewards
- consequences.

It is vital with new students and classes that careless assumptions are not made. Teachers who wish students to conform to their expectations must teach these requirements to their students and remember that behaviour is an important area of the curriculum:

- Teach behavioural expectations and boundaries. Be absolutely explicit. Leave no room for misinterpretation.
- Check to ensure that all students understand fully what is expected of them.
- Practice.
- Review on a regular basis.
- Constantly refer to these expectations.
- Have them permanently displayed in the teaching area, in both word and visual representation.
- Reward those who comply.

Environmental issues

Behaviour is closely linked to thoughts and feelings. People's impressions affect their emotions and that is also true of the impression created by the teaching environment. So ensure that the classroom is organised and decorated in such a way that it becomes a positive influence on students' behaviour. Spend some time at the beginning of the first week noting all the areas of the teaching space that need attention. Treat this period as a time for going through the 'snagging' list and take the students' views into consideration.

Teachers in situ can rectify some of the problems. Other problems, however, will need reporting to the caretaker or school management. Lighting, storage, appropriate seating, heating and learning resources are all essential ingredients in providing a learning environment that promotes a feeling of well-being.

The start of any new year or term is also a time for teachers to reacquaint themselves with the whole school approach to managing behaviour. Spend some time becoming familiar with the school handbook, reward systems and the sanctions used. Also devote some time to reviewing how contact is maintained with parents.

One of the most important points, as highlighted in the SEAL materials, is that behaviour can be 'caught' as well as taught. Teachers and students alike have had a lengthy break from the behavioural expectations of school. During this time everyone may have behaved in ways that would perhaps not have been appropriate in a school setting, and have enjoyed their time in a less structured environment. Once term has started, the school's

 This page may be photocopied for instructional use only. © Dave Stott (text) and Bill Stott (illustrations).

expectations kick in again. The teacher is once again in charge in the classroom and must reset the boundaries. Likewise, the students are once again subject to the teacher's guidance. In this way, teachers resume their role as important and influential figures in their students' lives. The teacher is the role model whose behaviour will be watched carefully, analysed and acted upon by a whole class of young people. In order for this to be effective from day one, the message is quite clear – do not expect this to happen as if by magic. It needs careful planning and forethought.

Top Tip 24

Always plan for the new school year

 This page may be photocopied for instructional use only. © Dave Stott (text) and Bill Stott (illustrations).

Non-verbal communication

Possibly the best place to observe non-verbal instruction in action is during a primary school assembly. The whole school is seated in the hall, children are in class group rows and the staff are seated down the sides of the hall. Non-verbal instructions or signals can be observed throughout the assembly. Teachers will be using 'the look' to maintain order amongst their group. This look 'wills' the misbehaving student into turning and looking at the teacher. The non-verbal instruction comes from the teacher's eyes, which are staring and fixed on the target student. This is accompanied by a familiar one-finger instruction as follows:

- The pointing finger indicates to where the target student should move.
- The index finger over the lips means 'be quiet'.
- The index finger raised vertically and curling towards the teacher, means 'come here'.
- The index finger outstretched vertically and swaying to and fro means 'No. Don't you dare!'

There might be several other, less pleasant, signals that could be observed, but those listed above are probably the most common. Even the youngest children quickly understand the meaning behind such non-verbal directions and will generally comply with them. Unfortunately, most non-verbal instructions remain very general and often negative. If it is true that in most cases children understand non-verbal instructions and do indeed comply with them, there is a very strong case for refining this system of communication and extending its use. Non-verbal communication has many benefits, including:

- saving the teacher's voice
- allowing the teacher to manage situations without embarrassment and the attention of peers that often accompanies verbal instructions
- allowing the teacher to tailor specific non-verbal instructions to individual students
- giving the teacher a unique style, which students often enjoy and which can strengthen the teacher–student relationship
- creating more stages (particularly low-level) within a class behaviour policy and preventing situations escalating to high-level responses and subsequent use of consequences
- allowing instructions to be given in a group without causing unnecessary disruption to the event taking place.

Non-verbal instructions or signals fall into the following three categories:

1   instructions and signals that are used consistently and on a whole school basis

2   instructions and signals that teachers use specifically for their own teaching groups in addition to those used for the whole school

3   instructions and signals that have been jointly agreed and developed with individual students, in addition to those used class-wide and for the whole school.

Many staff already use some of the above and will no doubt have devised a range of additional signals that are personal to their class group. However, it is vital that, to aid understanding, signs and signals intended for whole school use should be used consistently by all staff. Instructions and signals devised by teachers for use in their own classroom, and for individual students, should be taught in the same manner as any other part of the curriculum:

- Teach precisely the actions that will be used, and the response that is expected.
- Check for understanding by asking students questions about the instructions.
- Practise the instructions with the students, rewarding appropriate responses.
- Repeat the above stages regularly and, if possible, use visual (written and pictorial) reminders in the classroom.

A typical and well-used example of a non-verbal instruction to gain the attention of a group of students would be the following. The adult raises the right arm in the air, meaning students should:

- stop talking
- put things down

 This page may be photocopied for instructional use only. © Dave Stott (text) and Bill Stott (illustrations).

- look at the teacher.
- Students should also raise their right arms both to indicate understanding and to remind those who are not yet complying.

Clearly, this technique will work only if it has been taught to the students.

As mentioned, there are many such non-verbal signals that can be used and teachers are encouraged to devise some of their own. These techniques often prove even more effective if they are devised jointly with students. This is particularly relevant if the technique is intended for use with an individual student.

Share with other teachers

Another important point is to share these special signals with colleagues. Whenever a colleague has to cover a class, it is good practice for them to be able to retain the same systems and routines that have already been established, thereby minimising the disruption that the absence of the regular teacher may otherwise cause.

Teachers should be inventive when devising non-verbal instructions. The best starting point is a list of all the occasions for which voice is currently used. Students appreciate a novel approach to behaviour management and are more likely to remember the instructions. There should also be an equal number of positive and negative signals: there is a danger that teachers may develop a whole range of signals to remind students when they are off task, but use only a simple 'thumbs up' as a reward.

Rest the voice

 This page may be photocopied for instructional use only. © Dave Stott (text) and Bill Stott (illustrations).

Non-verbal reinforcement

Children begin to learn and understand the complicated signs and signals of non-verbal communication from a very early age. They experience, quite early on in life, encouraging smiles, the 'I know what you are doing' look and the slight frown that may indicate mild displeasure. These types of non-verbal communication are used to guide children through the maze of what is expected of them with regard to their everyday behaviour and social interactions. When non-verbal signs are coupled with verbal instructions or positive comments, then communication becomes more powerful.

The concept of non-verbal reinforcement continues right through the school years and into adulthood. Non-verbal reinforcement is increasingly evident on every high street throughout the community. Examples include the LED devices by the roadside that flash the driver's speed, reinforced with a 'smiley' or a 'sad face' (reward/sanction); and the 'smiley faces' that are used near bank counters to encourage customers to stand back and give others their privacy. The same types of device are used in all kinds of situations where a friendly, but firm, instruction is given to the public. Perhaps this overuse means that the impact will eventually be lost, but children do respond to non-verbal signs and signals, as seen by their use in the curriculum at Key Stage 1.

Schools already use all kinds of non-verbal communication, such as students' charters, school policies and classroom rules. More often than not, these all appear as written documents. Rules are accessed through websites and school handbooks and are also displayed on classroom noticeboards. This is fine for students who are able to read and for those who take the trouble to look, but they are not so effective for the rest of the school population. Teachers will sympathise with anyone attempting to verbally reinforce rules or expectations, because they often have to be repeated time and time again. When these rules are repeated so frequently, students suddenly become quite expert at employing selective hearing techniques.

Presentation is key

As just mentioned, in the average school most rules or expectations are presented as written documents. Some are presented in a drab and uncommunicative manner, whilst others employ large and colourful type. Not many of these same rules and expectations are reinforced by the use of signs or symbols or pictorial representation.

- Ask students to design posters to convey school or classroom rules visually, without the use of words. They should use only pictorial representation.
- Talk with the students about how the rules can be 'marketed' in a way that is understood by their peers. Use stickers, emails, badges, wristbands or other marketing materials. The results could be both surprising and innovative.

P This page may be photocopied for instructional use only. © Dave Stott (text) and Bill Stott (illustrations).

Tip 26

The use of relevant and eye-catching visual material that does not rely solely on the use of written language can be powerful and effective in reinforcing the rules, boundaries and reward systems in a school environment. For many young people it is more effective, and most certainly less confrontational, than verbal reminders. Visual or non-verbal reminders also have the benefit of being always 'on show', even when teachers are not present!

It is important to be aware that, like verbal reinforcement, the effectiveness will be greatly reduced by familiarity. To maintain the same initial impact or interest level, all the marketing materials need to be changed and updated on a regular basis. Each time they are changed they can be relaunched in much the same way as any common high street product. This approach could create excellent project work for art classes or business modules where marketing is part of the curriculum.

As a starter to using non-verbal reinforcement and reducing the use of word-based materials, try the following:

- Write out the classroom rules and then include visual interpretations.
- Do the same for all the verbal reinforcement statements. Be more imaginative than simply using smiley or sad faces: perhaps a cartoon character can be created.

- Design or purchase non-verbal posters for particular areas of the classroom or school (for example: reading area, library, corridors) that reinforce the expectations for the use of that area. (Everyone is familiar with the male/female/disability images used on toilet doors.)
- Monitor the behaviour of the young people using the targeted areas before and after displaying the posters.

The intention is to improve the behaviour of the young people and create a stimulating but reinforcing environment. Most importantly, this system will provide the teacher with effective, low-level behaviour management tools, thus reducing the need to use constant verbal and written reinforcement.

Top Tip 26

Use the students' artistic skills

 This page may be photocopied for instructional use only. © Dave Stott (text) and Bill Stott (illustrations).

Observing student behaviour

Every student with behaviour problems is a useful source of information. Clear and structured observations can provide feedback on the efficacy of Individual Education Plans or classroom management strategies. Individual information, such as time, place and task, can be collated with information on a number of other individual students, allowing teachers to observe patterns and similarities. This in turn will contribute to individual reviews and reveal any strengths and weaknesses of current arrangements. To avoid information overload, it is best to restrict this observation to no more than 10 students over any one period.

If discernable patterns do not emerge, and if each individual student's problems are quite specific, this more than likely indicates that the whole school approach is working well. However, if these observations show that all students are experiencing problems at, say, lunchtime, change of lesson or the start of the day, staff should consider whether there is a need to change whole school arrangements and policy at those particular times.

For individual students, collecting information about their behaviour allows teachers to formulate a working hypothesis about the nature of their problem. It is rarely possible to get it absolutely right at the beginning and teachers should be prepared to modify their arrangements as more information is collected.

Another vital link in collecting information about a problem is that any data collected before a programme begins can be used as a yardstick to decide whether the programme is being successful. In the absence of any measure of success, both teacher and student may feel like giving up because it appears that no progress has been made. With clear data, small steps are there for everyone – the teacher, the student, parents and the rest of the staff – to see.

Observing and collecting information is clearly useful, but can be incredibly time-consuming. As is the case with any intervention, the principle of using the 'first seen' response applies. There is a temptation to make endless and copious notes on a student's behaviour, only to find that this information is so overloaded that it is not very valuable. Too much information can be as harmful as too little. To be effective and useful the information-collecting process should be a fairly simple and straightforward operation.

By the end of the observation and data-collection process, clarity should be brought to the following questions:

- What exactly is the behaviour problem and what exactly would it be preferable for the student to be doing instead?
- When and under what circumstances is the behaviour most likely to occur?
- What seems to be happening after the behaviour has occurred that may be causing it to continue?

 This page may be photocopied for instructional use only. © Dave Stott (text) and Bill Stott (illustrations).

Tip 27

Collecting information

Start by collecting simple information on a number of problems and deciding which problem is the one to start with. The simplest approach would be to record:

- What?
- When?
- Why?
- Where?

Once it has been decided which problems need to be worked on further, there are a number of different methods that can be used to collect the required information. These will depend on the behaviour to be recorded and the time and resources available.

- Event or incident recording. This is probably the simplest method of collecting information about a behaviour problem. Use a diary to collect information on events that do not occur too frequently. The diary should be used to record specific incidents rather than lengthy descriptions of general behaviour. Include information about the setting, where and when it took place, and the outcome. It is important to report the teacher's actions and the student's response. This system is often known as ABC recording (Antecedent, Behaviour and Consequence).

- Frequency or tally recording. The type of recording just described can be adapted to record priority behaviour problems that occur more frequently. As well as noting general information, a tally should be kept of the frequency. Make decisions about whether it is best to reduce the frequency or eliminate the behaviour altogether. There are also some health and safety issues to consider. Shouting out in class may be reduced, but kicking other students must be eliminated as soon as possible.

- Ratio recording. The tally technique can be refined to provide a ratio measure which takes into account the opportunities that arose for a behaviour to occur, as well as the number of times it actually happened. This will give a more accurate picture of the problem.

- Duration recording. The duration of an incident is recorded. This form of recording should only be used when simply counting the number of times an incident occurs would give a false picture of the problem.

- Time sampling. When a behaviour occurs frequently or continues for a long time, event or duration recording may prove too time-consuming. Time sampling involves observing a student either at random or at fixed intervals and noting whether the behaviour is occurring at the time of observation.

Changes in the attitude of students with persistent behaviour problems can often be small. Good record keeping will help in the planning of appropriate interventions and also demonstrate progress to all concerned.

Top Tip 27

Make use of good data collection

 This page may be photocopied for instructional use only. © Dave Stott (text) and Bill Stott (illustrations).

Off task but not disrupting

For some teachers and teaching assistants, the temptation to ignore students who are not actually disrupting anyone, but are clearly not involved with the lesson, is overwhelming. They operate on the basis of 'If you're not bothering me, then I won't bother you.' This attitude often comes from despair or frustration and quite often because the teacher has run out of ideas on how to deal with the student in question.

There may be occasions when it might be appropriate to 'tactically ignore' the student for a short time, but this practice should be used sparingly. Everyone needs space and it may well be that a particular student should be given a little leeway from time to time. Time-limited and closely monitored tactical ignoring can be an effective strategy. However, this should not be confused with allowing the student to become, over a period of time, disengaged from the learning environment.

If allowed to continue, off-task students who are currently not disrupting quickly learn that the teacher is quite happy for them to waste time and will subsequently find it difficult to follow instructions and maintain concentration. These same students, when not refocused, often change into an off-task and very disruptive mode. Students who are allowed to continue their off-task behaviour are often the subject of taunts and jibes from their peers, have low self-esteem and may well go on to significantly underachieve.

Another unwanted side effect of permitting off-task behaviour is a lack of consistency among all students in the teaching group. This often leads to some disaffection and the dreaded statement made by those students who are redirected: 'It's not fair! John's not working, so why should I?'

Teachers should be aware that, even though the student is not overtly bothering anyone, this behaviour pattern can have an impact on the teacher's own feelings and eventually the behaviour of the group as a whole.

All teachers have experienced the moment when they are teaching a class group, scanning all the students, and suddenly notice that someone is off task. This can lead to a variety of feelings, which the teacher needs to be able to manage. Such feelings include the anxiety caused by not knowing how to respond or, even worse, the stress caused by knowing only too well what will happen if or when the response is made. It is vital, at this point, that teachers have well-rehearsed and effective strategies that should be used in a graded and gradual approach. In this way, teachers will become proficient in assessing the situation quickly and engaging the student at the lowest possible level of intervention.

Name dropping

Everybody is tuned into their own name – generally their first name. A good low-level and non-intrusive method of bringing the off-task student 'back into the room' is simply to use their name in the next instruction or conversation. Do not use it in a patronising or derogative way; just slip the name into a sentence. Accompany this by moving closer to the student concerned. This is such a simple strategy, but is certainly one that develops into a powerful motivator every time. At the same time, remember that the intention is to re-engage the student, not to make them look 'silly' or embarrass them in front of their friends.

Be aware of personal space. When moving closer to the student, it is vitally important to understand that the teacher's proximity has a strong effect on the student. The speed of approach, body language and final proximity will determine either how successful the teacher is in getting the student back on task or, at worst, what sort of confrontation is being encouraged. Simply standing closer to the student and continuing the lesson will be sufficient to act as a reminder to that student to get back on task.

Don't forget that the teacher who is operating at a high level of awareness will always offer a reward, be it verbal or non-verbal, to the student who complies. Be careful to make the reward simple, effective and, most importantly, age appropriate.

Top Tip 28

Utilise tactical thinking

 This page may be photocopied for instructional use only. © Dave Stott (text) and Bill Stott (illustrations).

One-to-one conversations

Imagine the following as a typical scenario: the teacher is half way through the second lesson on a Monday morning. The class have been restless and the constant low-level disruptions have stretched to the limit the patience and management skills of both teacher and assistant. Neither was prepared for this class. This period would normally have been non-contact time. Instead, these members of staff were in front of a class covering for an absent colleague and dealing with a group of students who were also unhappy with the situation.

Familiar? This scenario is one that has been repeated in many schools over the years and most teachers will recognise it and empathise with the emotions it generates. Anger, frustration and a general feeling of self-pity can all contribute to an out-of-character response that may follow. This response is usually a 'build-up' (liken it to a volcano) and it is at this point that teachers should use a range of strategies to calm down, distract the students or move on and tactically ignore the problems. The danger is that it may catch the teacher unawares and result in a confrontation that is damaging in both the short and the long term to both teacher and student alike.

When a teacher, or indeed any person, is feeling stressed or challenged, it is extremely difficult to think and act in a controlled and logical manner. Something as simple as a passing comment, an expression or a direct challenge can tip the balance and allow the volcano to erupt. It is quite clearly not the appropriate time to take up a long and often confrontational conversation with a student, and yet many teachers do this at some time. While feeling out of sorts, it is only too easy for the teacher to be drawn into an argument which the student quite clearly relishes. The teacher may be quite aware that the rest of the class is not only watching but could also take sides and join in. In this situation the teacher will find little support.

So before things get as far as this it is essential that teachers have a clear and planned strategy that enables them to:

- cope with the immediate problem
- present a consistent and united role model with any other adult in the classroom
- demonstrate to all students that their behaviour will not be tolerated
- demonstrate that even if they choose not to enter into a conversation right now, the issue will be dealt with at a later time and on the teacher's terms.

Self-calming strategies, sharing the problem with the teaching assistant and having a clear 'behaviour plan' are vital ingredients when faced with the situation just described. Sometimes the simplest solutions are the most effective. Perhaps it is the teacher who is causing the problem. If teacher and teaching assistant have a good working relationship, this may be an opportune time for them to swap roles – far better for the latter to intervene and allow the teacher to calm down and get on with something else. This may well solve the confrontation problem.

Any teacher who finds themselves drawn into this type of situation should consider the following steps:

- Risk-assess the situation. Does the teacher really need to get involved?
- Use self-calming strategies before intervening.
- If there is another adult in the room consider asking that person to intervene.
- Move closer to the student and use the planned approach. A graded and gradual model of intervention that gives the student opportunities to make choices about their behaviour will help.
- Do not engage in a lengthy verbal altercation.

Problem solving

The next step is to consider speaking to the student about their behaviour in a situation that is:

- removed from the present situation and not in the presence of classmates
- calm, fair and planned
- not used as an opportunity to blame or reprimand the student, but as a problem-solving conversation.

 This page may be photocopied for instructional use only. © Dave Stott (text) and Bill Stott (illustrations).

The teacher should state clearly the nature of the problem and explain why that particular episode was unacceptable: 'John, I can't let you continually chat during my lesson. You are disrupting the other students, and I am not prepared to let you answer me back when I remind you.' The intention of the meeting is to express concerns, explain why the behaviour was a problem and, perhaps more importantly, allow both student and teacher to have the opportunity of talking without the worry of peer pressure or the anger that may have been present initially.

Always attempt to conclude the meeting with some solutions. It is important that a positive and encouraging experience is conveyed. The teacher should agree what they are going to do and what the student should try to do in order to avoid a repeat of the situation. Keep a record of these meetings and the outcomes. Such information will be useful at any future reviews of the student's behaviour. Also make sure that a member of staff is aware of the meeting and that the behaviour policy of the school is being respected.

TopTip 29

Meet with the student

P This page may be photocopied for instructional use only. © Dave Stott (text) and Bill Stott (illustrations).

Passive and aggressive adult behaviour

When dealing with behaviour management issues in the teaching and learning environment, the importance of the adult as a role model should not be underestimated. Teachers who have been introduced to and have practised self-calming techniques will understand the importance of managing their own emotions before attempting to deal with a difficult group or individual student. For the student looking to 'push buttons' or to disrupt the concentration of fellow students, the teacher's own attitude and self-control is highly influential.

- A passive tone of voice that is almost whining and often interspersed with 'tutting' or exasperated sighs.
- Palms of the hands are that are open with arms out straight in a questioning stance.
- Shrugging the shoulders whilst looking skywards and shaking the head from side to side, thus giving a non-verbal 'No, no, no' message.

More than 75 per cent of communication is largely non-verbal, making not just what is said but how it is said a major contributory factor in providing a successful working environment for teachers and students alike. Verbal and non-verbal behaviour plays an important role in the building of strong and effective relationships with the student group. Teachers who feel constantly under pressure and stressed, due to the challenging behaviour of their students, begin to question their own professional abilities. Under these circumstances it is difficult for them to enjoy teaching, and both their health and well-being are undermined by the constant pressure.

Neither passive nor aggressive behaviour displayed by the teaching adult will lessen the pressure that they feel in their day-to-day contact with students. Neither type of behaviour will gain the respect or cooperation of their students and will more likely lead to a worsening of the situation. The first step here is to recognise the typical traits of passive behaviour:

- Linked to all of the above is the final passive trait: moving close to the student and asking questions such as: 'How many times do I have to tell you …?' or 'Now what am I going to do with you?' The first question opens a dialogue with the student which, under these circumstances, is best avoided. The second question clearly demonstrates that the teacher does not have a clue about what to do next.

Passive behaviour, as described above, can quickly change into aggressive behaviour, particularly when the chosen passive strategy is inflaming the situation. Some teachers, however, do not go through the passive stage, but instead leap in immediately with aggression. This is how it looks:

- loud, threatening tone of voice, generally giving short, sharp direct instructions
- an aggressive body language with tense muscles, clenched fists, sweating, and so on

P This page may be photocopied for instructional use only. © Dave Stott (text) and Bill Stott (illustrations).

- an increased heart rate accompanied by a reddening face
- verbal comments that berate the student, leading to emotional outbursts and verbal abuse
- direct and fast movement towards the student with the resulting invasion of personal space
- overt physical behaviour such as banging the desk or slamming books down on the table.

This style of aggressive behaviour demonstrates to the student that the teacher is out of control and disregards the feelings of others. The lasting effect of both passive and aggressive behaviour on students is a total lack of respect for and belief in the teacher as a role model. At worst, it leaves the student with a sense of misplaced power over the teacher ('I enjoyed doing that to him, let's try again!') or, on the other hand, a deep-seated fear. Both are unhealthy outcomes.

Work with colleagues

Every teacher has a preferred style of management. It is nevertheless important that teachers should be self-critical and take some time to reflect on their own techniques. Does the teacher have any of the above-mentioned traits in their classroom management routines? It might be worthwhile at this point to consult with a colleague to help identify any idiosyncrasy or attitude that may be seen by others as passive or aggressive.

Any teacher who works regularly with a teaching assistant already has a built-in analyst. In this situation it is easy to set up a two-way process where each adult in the classroom can help the other. Here are some specific points that are worth looking at closely:

- Facial expression: does the face go bright red in certain situations?
- Use of language: does the teacher ask lots of questions? Does the teacher always give direct and forceful directions whilst not expecting a reply?
- Body language: look at the overall body posture. Are the arms folded? Are the shoulders hunched, dropped, tight, tense or almost too upright?
- Speed of approach: does the teacher advance rapidly and invade students' personal space?
- Teachers could measure their resting heart rate and compare it to their heart rate whilst teaching. What does it rise to when dealing with a difficult situation? The easiest way to check the heart rate is with a heart-rate monitor. The resting rate can be found first thing in the morning: check it again mid-morning and mid-afternoon whilst teaching.
- Ask a colleague to write down exactly what was said during an altercation with a student. Was the verbal language overly passive or clearly aggressive?

Every teacher will utilise behaviour patterns that fall neatly into either passive or aggressive modes at some time during the working day. Do, however, be aware just how much the teacher's attitude can affect the students' own behaviour. No teacher can be a perfect paragon of good behaviour but, as the role model, the teacher must remain in control of thoughts and emotions. This is because these thoughts and emotions drive their behaviour and ultimately influence the behaviour of the students in their care.

Be self-critical

 This page may be photocopied for instructional use only. © Dave Stott (text) and Bill Stott (illustrations).

50 Top Tips
for Managing Behaviour

Peer pressure

A frequent remark in the staffroom is that a particular child is fine on their own but quite a different person when in a class group. Many young people, both within educational establishments and elsewhere, are vulnerable to pressure from their peers. Despite increasing awareness of social skills and emotional literacy, there is a strong tendency for individuals to 'follow the group'. Even the strongest-willed individuals can find themselves carried along by the general demeanour of the class and exhibiting behaviours that they would never exhibit when on their own.

It is not solely that young people do not want to be seen as the one who does not quite fit in with the group. Some children are extremely vulnerable to pressure from others for many different reasons, whilst others enjoy exerting influence on the 'weaker' members of the class. This is a major problem for classroom management and one that can prove to be a significant contributory factor in student misbehaviour and teacher stress.

When asked to identify how many students with behavioural difficulties are present in their classroom, many teachers typically name, for example, 10 to 12 students in a teaching group of 28 to 32. This means that teachers may recognise almost half their group as 'difficult' or 'challenging'. However, if the same class

group were to be viewed rationally by an outside consultant, the number of difficult students would be placed at somewhere between two and five. The difference in the two figures quoted here results from the peer pressure that persuades many young people to follow colleagues in their behaviour patterns. This increases the perceived numbers of difficult students in the average classroom.

Students are faced with unrelenting, and often severe, pressure to gain the approval or win the respect of their fellow classmates. The student who can successfully antagonise the teacher or make the whole class laugh gains considerable credibility from their actions. Anyone who chooses not to join in leaves themselves open to verbal and sometimes physical abuse. They can be ridiculed and even bullied by other group members. Under these circumstances it takes an exceptionally strong and confident individual to stand out from the crowd.

It is very much easier to deal with unacceptable peer pressure in a generally relaxed and well-behaved classroom, where there are likely to be only a few incidents to cope with. However, if the majority of the group is constantly misbehaving and the number of difficult students really is 10 to 12, teachers will be faced with an extremely difficult proposition.

P This page may be photocopied for instructional use only. © Dave Stott (text) and Bill Stott (illustrations).

Interestingly, positive peer pressure has been used for many years in the classroom, and some behaviour management programmes promote the technique. Used wisely, discreetly organised positive pressure can counter much of the negative pressure that comes from the wilful few. Strategies that are currently being used in classrooms can be as simple as:

- 'Let's see who is ready. Good. Everyone on table 3 is sitting up ready to go out!' The clear message here is that if the group on table 3 is ready, there is no reason why the other tables should not be ready too. After all, they are no different.

- Well done group 2, everyone is looking at me and ready to start!' Again, the message, although directed at group 2, is intended as pressure on those who have not complied with the request.

In both these examples the teacher is relying on students needing praise for complying with the instruction. Those who are complying receive the praise, and peer pressure encourages the rest to follow.

When faced with peer pressure from students, teachers can quickly become defensive, stressed and in a general state of panic. It is easy for teachers to find themselves 'hooked' by distraction techniques or goaded into shouting at students in an effort to control a skirmish in the classroom. Peer pressure can easily result in an increase in the numbers of students involved. Some students find it difficult to resist being sucked into the action. When this happens, the initial small group rapidly escalates into whole class disorder. This is where both proactive and reactive tactics are required.

Proactive tactics

- Consider restructuring the classroom. Rearrange the seating and ensure that equipment is easily accessible. It might be viewed as unfair to seat difficult students next to those who are well behaved, but as a short-term strategy it is better than allowing the misbehaviour to continue.

- Teachers should continually rehearse classroom styles until their own behaviour becomes planned, structured and controlled.

- Teachers are encouraged to take a long hard look at lesson timings and what they are expecting the students to undertake in any given session.

- During lessons keep students engaged and interested.

- Revisit the class-wide behaviour and discipline plans.

- Ensure that students are taught how to resist peer pressure.

Reactive tactics

- Be positive, focus on those who are behaving well and following instructions.

- Use the class behaviour plan consistently and do not be afraid to impose class-wide sanctions.

- Have one-to-one meetings with the most difficult students. Plan the conversation, hold it away from an audience and make sure it happens when all parties have calmed down.

- Do not remain seated at a desk throughout the lesson: mingle with the class group and ensure that all students receive equal time.

- Use first names when scanning the classroom. Always look for opportunities to use age-appropriate praise.

Top Tip 31

Teach students how to say 'no'

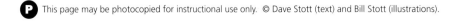
P This page may be photocopied for instructional use only. © Dave Stott (text) and Bill Stott (illustrations).

Plenary evaluations

Students are usually only too happy to pick up their kit at the end of a lesson and rapidly move on to the next event. Teachers quite often experience a sense of relief as the lesson draws to a close so that they can recover and prepare for the next session – this is particularly true if the class has been difficult to manage.

The problem with just rushing off to the next thing is that events are not discussed and issues are not resolved. It is far better to spend just five minutes with the students at the end of each lesson to gain a clear and objective picture of both students' and teacher's feelings about the session. Establishing this student feedback after the end of each lesson is a powerful (and subtle) approach to behaviour management. Such evaluation is common practice on teacher training courses, and it is therefore not unreasonable to extend this experience to the classroom.

The information that this approach generates will enable the teacher to work in a positive environment. This will minimise the risk of off-task or confrontational behaviour, especially if the teacher pays attention to the feedback from the most troubled students. Plenary evaluations give both teacher and student alike the opportunity to reflect on the lesson, consider how everyone felt, and more importantly, discover what can be learned and applied to the next session.

Plenary evaluation is a skill that has to be developed, and students will need to learn how to participate in a

responsible way. Do not allow a one-off incident or the opinion of a small group of students to mislead the class regarding the overall success of the lesson. Teachers should ensure that the evaluation takes place on a variety of levels, particularly when attempting to gain a clear picture of their own behaviour management skills. This checklist is a good starting point:

- Gain an overall impression of the lesson.
- Look at techniques and strategies used in response to individual students.
- Observe the techniques and strategies used for groups.
- Listen to students' own observations.
- Encourage contributions from any support staff in the room.

Plenary evaluations do not need to be time-consuming. The last five minutes of any lesson can be usefully spent in finishing off activities, putting away equipment and discussing, both formally and informally, how students feel about the lesson. This approach links in to the five domains of the Social and Emotional Aspects of Learning (SEAL) initiative:

1   **Recognising emotions**. What impact did the session and everyone's behaviour have on the emotions of both teacher and students?
2   **Managing feelings**. What strategies were used during the lesson?

P This page may be photocopied for instructional use only. © Dave Stott (text) and Bill Stott (illustrations).

3 Motivation. Were goals set and a successful outcome planned?

4 Empathy. Were the feelings and needs of others considered?

5 Social skills. Were people able to apply these skills in a group environment?

The effect of plenary evaluations on overall behaviour can be very powerful. This is because these sessions allow teachers to express their own observations to their students, whilst demonstrating that they also consider it important enough to listen to students' observations.

A much more simple approach to evaluation can be used with younger students. At the close of a lesson simply ask the class to indicate how they felt. Encourage a very easily understood response, such as the following:

- Ask the children to use a 'thumbs up', 'thumbs down' or 'thumbs sideways' sign to indicate their feelings.

- Use 'smiley' or 'sad faces'. This could be varied by children using their own facial expressions, pictures or even masks.

Act on the feedback

For some groups it might be more effective to ask for signs or to make observations at regular intervals during the lesson, rather than waiting until the end. Use a 15-minute timer, temporarily halt the activities and ask for instant feedback: 'How is everyone on table one feeling? What about table two?' Use these opportunities to check whether the students are having any problems. Be aware of and responsive to the work atmosphere. If the students are deeply engrossed in a particular activity, it may not be wise to interrupt and ask for feedback!

For older students, the same basic criteria will apply. Use the plenary evaluations to:

- adopt a proactive behaviour management style

- demonstrate to the students that their observations are important

- learn from the students' comments

- give everyone a fair opportunity to air their views in a safe environment

- allow students to see and understand how individual behaviour can affect the dynamics of the group.

The 'thumbs up', 'thumbs down' system described earlier may also be used for older students in certain situations. At other times a more formal method can be used to provide more in-depth information. It is important always to seek student involvement by, for example, designing a purpose-made evaluation form in consultation with the students. This need not be complicated because the plenary session should take no more than five minutes. The feedback received should be used to reflect on and/or change the behaviour and approach of both students and teacher. It is imperative that teachers include themselves in all feedback sessions and they must be prepared to answer any important points that arise. Finally, these feedback opportunities enable teachers to adjust their teaching style in response to observations and this will benefit all concerned.

Top Tip 32

Learn from students' comments

P This page may be photocopied for instructional use only. © Dave Stott (text) and Bill Stott (illustrations).

Proactive and positive

Events outside of the classroom can affect how an individual student behaves during the day. Problems at home with family or with another student on the way to school can set a scene where a student is disturbed or distracted for the rest of the day. This can be more applicable to some students than others. It is difficult, if not impossible, to ask a student to leave their emotional 'baggage' outside the school gates. Teachers therefore need to recognise that these outside events can influence a student's ability to learn in class.

This alone highlights teachers' importance as role models for appropriate behaviour and how influential they can be in the classroom. Teachers should be able to recognise the signs displayed by individual students and be emotionally prepared to engage with and motivate them. This needs careful planning, well-practised skills and good strategic thinking. Teachers also need to manage their own emotions carefully in order to stay on top of these situations and be of real help to the students concerned.

There is no point in waiting for problems to develop and then trying to work out what caused the difficulty, find the appropriate reaction and come up with an instant strategy that is based on hope rather than experience. This style of approach simply demonstrates to the student that the teacher is ill-prepared, unlikely to treat them as an individual, and does not work within clearly thought-out boundaries and guidelines. Many students will then spend the rest of their time with that teacher testing, probing and 'pressing buttons' to see just how far they can go.

The day ahead does not depend simply on the 'baggage' that the student brings into the school: it is also clearly dependent on the emotional and professional preparedness of the teaching staff. It is far easier for a mature adult to leave their problems at the school gate than it is for students. Given the emotional background of the average teaching day, how can teachers ensure that they maintain a positive and proactive teaching style?

In order to stand any chance of being calm, professional and proactive in their working environment, teachers need to take time to plan and prepare. Preparation is the strength that teachers need so that issues that would normally affect their mood or emotional equilibrium are negated. Perhaps the day starts as follows:

- Out of bed late, the car will not start, the weather is appalling and the post contains bad news.

- Furthermore, it is Monday morning and the day starts with an 'unnecessary' staff briefing.
- The problem class is due to be taught just after lunch.

If these issues grow in stature, the teacher may begin to focus on all the negative aspects of the day ahead. By the time the classroom is reached, this negativity will be apparent and will affect the way the teacher interacts with students and colleagues. This is hardly the way to deliver positive messages to students, who will be very quick to pick up on the atmosphere created and the body language conveyed. Under these circumstances think about:

- the messages that facial expression and body posture convey
- the impact that the negative facial expression and poor body posture have on the class group – remember here that behaviour can be 'caught' as well as taught.

Notwithstanding the depressing start to the day, taking a positive view can quickly lift the clouds of despair. So it is worth passing the school gate with a smile and then to:

- make positive or encouraging comments to students
- make a conscious effort each day to give positive and sincere statements to colleagues
- remember that the sincerity and the effectiveness of these remarks will be judged not just against the content of what is said, but also by the tone of voice, body posture, eye contact and facial expression.

Planning is key

Few successful teachers begin a lesson without a lesson plan. A lesson plan enables them to ensure that learning styles are catered for and the work is differentiated, recognising the needs of individual students. This same planned approach is also applied to proactive behaviour management. When teachers have spent time creating a positive mood and working environment, they must also be prepared for more challenging situations:

- Make sure there are more than one or two steps in any response to challenging situations. If responses are not well rehearsed, graded and gradual in style, it is only too easy to revert quickly to threats and a challenging (or passive) behavioural management style.

 This page may be photocopied for instructional use only. © Dave Stott (text) and Bill Stott (illustrations).

- Developing a partnership with one or more colleagues is a way of placing emotional literacy and staff well-being within the ethos of the school. Work with colleagues to regularly practise management styles and approaches.

- Put emotional literacy at the top of the agenda within the staff group by regularly rating emotions and feelings following staff meetings, lessons, the lunch break, and so on. Use a simple rating system, such as 1 = awful, 10 = brilliant.

Before teachers can truly begin to nurture and develop the behavioural skills and emotional literacy of the young people they work with, they need to develop as role models themselves. Recognising and understanding their own emotions is a valuable step towards that objective.

TopTip33

Leave emotional baggage at the school gate

P This page may be photocopied for instructional use only. © Dave Stott (text) and Bill Stott (illustrations).

Recognising early warning signs

'He just went for it, flew off the handle!' How many times has this statement been repeated when people are discussing another's anger? Do individuals really just 'lose it' without warning? It is important for teachers to understand and recognise the triggers that cause anger to develop in the first place and then have the skills or strategies to manage it. This applies equally to students, and both teachers and students should have the ability to recognise the early warning signs.

It is rare for the 'fuse' of developing anger to be lit without warning and for it to burn without the opportunity for intervention. When people say that another person 'just exploded', they are really saying that they themselves did not see the triggers and were not aware of all the clues as to how the individual was feeling during the lead-up to the incident. Naturally, this lead-up time can vary tremendously and sometimes it can be very short. But the clues and signs will always be there.

Many potentially angry situations can be contained successfully by providing a teaching and learning environment that recognises the individual needs of all concerned. Seating plans, appropriate activities and positive relationships between students and adults can negate the need to manage anger. Under these circumstances opportunities for anger rarely arise. If they do, however, it is important to remember that anger is a perfectly normal emotion. It is how it is managed that is key. Two pieces of advice are particularly relevant in the management of anger. They can be summed up as:

- prevention rather than cure
- proactive rather than reactive.

Early warning signs can vary from individual to individual. The teacher's role in the classroom is to know the individual student, become familiar with their signs and signals, and teach them some management strategies of their own. Once the individual signs have been noted and recognised, the information should be recorded and made available to everyone who works with that particular student. This would normally form part of the general information about a student and may be included in an Individual Education Plan or Pastoral Support Plan.

It is not possible to provide a comprehensive guide here to the early warning signs of imminent anger in all individuals. However, someone about to become angry may exhibit some, if not all, of the following signals:

- unusual body posture or change to their normal body posture (arms tightly folded, hands on hips)
- change in eye contact (continuous stare or refusal to engage in any eye contact)
- fidgeting (foot tapping, finger clicking, pen tapping on the desk – usually increasing in tempo and volume)
- sweating
- change in breathing (might be loud and noisy, accompanied by changes in facial expression)
- certain facial expressions (tight lipped or contorted)
- tension in the body (tight fists; tension in the neck, arms, jaw)
- change in verbal communication (refusal to engage in any form of verbal communication or muttering under the breath: this can often increase in volume very quickly)
- refusal to comply with instructions.

It is also possible to teach students to recognise the early warning signs themselves. Many young people do not relate the signs of temperature change or 'butterflies in the tummy' to imminent anger. Spend time talking to students and try to help them to identify their own feelings in different situations. Once they begin to recognise their own feelings and make the link between feelings/emotions and behaviour, it is then possible to equip them with effective strategies to manage their anger. It will also help them recognise developing anger in others.

Be open and discuss the issues

Visual reminders, such as a wall-mounted anger thermometer or a 'What makes me angry' chart, act as a permanent reminder to the class. Another way of doing this is to prepare a list, presented in both written and pictorial form, highlighting students' own feelings when they become angry – this will help them identify key triggers and warning signs.

For older students, one-to-one private meetings, held when neither party feels angry, are a very useful opportunity to discuss early warning signs, individual behaviour and effective management strategies. Provide a record of these discussions for the student and hold update meetings for as long as required. Evaluate the success of these sessions and be prepared to change tactics if necessary.

 This page may be photocopied for instructional use only. © Dave Stott (text) and Bill Stott (illustrations).

It is also worth noting that recognising early warning signs and having to hand appropriate strategies to manage anger is equally as applicable to all adults in a school as it is to all students. Teachers should recognise their own early warning signs: those who discuss these with other staff members are often surprised at how colleagues' observations differ from their own.

Top Tip 34

Plan – don't react!

℗ This page may be photocopied for instructional use only. © Dave Stott (text) and Bill Stott (illustrations).

IN THE 'FIGHT OR FLIGHT' SCENARIO, MR FITTOCK USUALLY OPTS FOR 'FAINT'

Responding to confrontation

People tend to have two automatic responses to confrontation, which are best summed up as 'fight' or 'flight'. These responses are thought to be inbuilt mechanisms to protect against either real or perceived threats. Unfortunately, they are hardly adequate when working with groups of students; teachers therefore need to find alternative strategies that work in the classroom. Challenging authority or 'pushing the buttons', for example, are activities enjoyed by some students. Using either of the responses just mentioned to deal with these, however, both limits the teacher's chances of successfully managing situations and demonstrates a poor role model to the students involved.

Self-calming techniques, such as deep breathing or counting to 10, are common suggestions that teachers may find useful when faced with confrontational behaviour. On their own, these 'pause' techniques are seldom a reliable means of avoiding the trouble that some students may actively seek. All adults working with young people in an educational setting should be seen as teachers of behaviour: professionals who provide environments in which appropriate behaviour is both taught and 'caught'. For this reason, it is important to work with students on strategies that prevent hostilities, rather than always being in a position of having to react to confrontation.

Teachers' reactions are determined entirely by how they feel at the time. It is worth noting that thoughts and feelings drive actions. This is why it is important to slow down when faced with a challenging or threatening situation. Consider the following:

- Teachers must try to recognise the problem they are facing and be aware of their own trigger points.
- Teachers should pause briefly before reacting in order both to compose body language and to decide what is going to be said or done. Remember that more than 80 per cent of all communication is non-verbal.
- Teachers should avoid getting drawn in.

For the teacher, school is their workplace. It is therefore as important for teachers as it is for students to create a working environment in which all participants feel confident, comfortable and supported. It is also important for teachers to feel in control and generally relaxed at school. To achieve this, an atmosphere of professional support must be created.

When more than one adult is involved in any confrontational situation, professional support can be vital. Quite often just a sideways glance, creating brief eye contact with another adult, can reduce tension.

 This page may be photocopied for instructional use only. © Dave Stott (text) and Bill Stott (illustrations).

Combine this with the kind of self-calming techniques mentioned above, and it becomes easier to take control.

Remember at this point that body language is the driver that can calm both student and teacher. The following actions will help:

- Stand in a neutral position: hands together in front of the body, fists unclenched and with palms facing downwards.
- Standing face-to-face can seem threatening, so stand slightly side on.
- Put the body weight on the back foot to avoid any aggressive forward-leaning posture.

These positions can become part of a 'muscle memory' and should be adopted automatically when the person concerned is faced with a confrontation or stressful situations. They can be psychologically linked to self-calming, help maintain confidence and also demonstrate to students good role modelling.

Do not become angry

Any verbal response should be carefully scripted. Do not ask questions, and avoid making accusations and 'blaming' statements. Consider carefully both the volume and tone of voice: two or more individuals in a confrontation will often try to voice match. Therefore if the teacher is loud and angry, it can only be expected that the student will try to equal this.

Keep instructions and statements clear and precise. Teachers should be aware that they must be prepared to act on anything they say. Students quickly recognise empty threats, and will push even further to see how far they can go. In any confrontational situation, remember that the first person who needs to calm down is the teacher. Indeed, as suggested above, the teacher should avoid getting angry and always remain calm. It is also important to keep the number of those involved as low as possible at all times. If another student tries to intervene, ask them, gently and with a smile, to sit down or leave the area. An angry response to anyone wishing to join in will only serve to escalate the situation.

Bear in mind at all times that when someone is confronted or threatened, the same fight/flight or hostile/passive feelings mentioned earlier will still occur, but most important is how those feelings are managed.

Top Tip 35

Avoid playing to an audience

 This page may be photocopied for instructional use only. © Dave Stott (text) and Bill Stott (illustrations).

Rewards

One of the five key domains in the Social and Emotional Aspects of Learning (SEAL) initiative is motivation. Different things drive different people and using a carefully planned reward system linked to behaviour rather than to academic achievement may well be the trigger to encourage some students to behave well. Rewards are often seen as school-wide motivators, but in this instance it is important to look at how to encourage good behaviour within the individual classroom.

Many children and young people have in-built skills necessary to enable them to be focused and motivated, even at the very earliest of ages. They realise the benefits of seeing a task through to its conclusion or abiding by the accepted guidelines and boundaries of expected behaviour. For these students, emotional and concrete rewards are less essential than for students who are easily distracted and cannot see the reasons for or benefits of working towards and within the set boundaries.

Students who are self-motivated nevertheless still need encouragement, praise and recognition. A brief look into some classrooms will invariably reveal that groups of students who do not habitually conform to the class rules or guidelines are the only students who ever receive rewards for improved behaviour. It is the student who presents no problem in the classroom who frequently goes unnoticed and is to a large extent ignored.

Whether rewards are used with individual students or on a class-wide basis, it is important that they are used clearly and consistently and in the form of a hierarchy. Both teacher and student should know what to expect. Start with the lowest form of reward available (this could be just an approving glance) and continue up the scale with a clear menu of available rewards. Ensure that these actually work: many teachers persist in using rewards they have used for years simply because that is the easiest option, yet there is no evidence that they actually work. Rewards are in place to motivate, encourage, improve confidence and raise self-esteem. If they fail on any or all of these counts, then it is time to rethink the strategy.

For a reward programme to be effective, it must be meaningful, consistent and used fairly. Students should be involved in the initial selection of rewards and also in any evaluation of their effectiveness. In this way, there is every possibility that they will be effective – students will actually like the rewards and therefore be motivated by them. Ensure at this stage that they do not conflict with national, county or school guidelines or with the cultural requirements of a particular student group.

Make sure that the reason for a reward being given is clear. There is no point in a student receiving rewards and praise for their ability to produce a good piece of work if their behaviour whilst working was totally unacceptable. Consider these two simple ideas to help students understand:

1 'Good, you have waited your turn to speak' is much better than just saying 'Good'.

2 Use stickers or rubber stamps, but make sure they indicate why they have been given. The 'well done' sticker may well be misinterpreted when taken out of context, so ensure that it answers the question 'For what?'

This page may be photocopied for instructional use only. © Dave Stott (text) and Bill Stott (illustrations).

Tip 36

As suggested above, also consider constructing a staged system of rewards that is graded and gradual. Ensure that rewards are age appropriate. At the early levels use non-verbal recognition, such as:

- signs and gestures (for example, 'thumbs up')
- a smile or a nod of approval
- proximity to the student

A flexible approach

Class-wide rewards can be very effective, especially where the 'target' student is the one responsible for earning the points. Peer pressure can be very powerful, as well as quite harmful in some cases. Careful management will keep this approach positive. However, if the use of a wider reward system proves to be counterproductive or it creates an uncomfortable feeling, this type of approach should not be used.

It is not easy to determine which rewards should be used or when they should be used. Every class group is different and needs tailored management, especially when dealing with behavioural issues. There are as many situations as there are individuals. So be flexible and learn through experience what works. Use the following guidelines to underpin the classroom approach:

- When agreeing rewards obtain input from all concerned.
- Be consistent in the application of rewards. Do not use them exclusively for one group of students. Set them out in a graded and gradual form, least to greatest.
- Display them and refer to them as often as possible.
- Evaluate and be prepared to change them if they are not working.
- Ensure that they work in the interest of all students.

Be positive, recognise good behaviour and always show approval. Remember to include all students in the programme. The overall effect will be better behaviour and improved self-esteem.

Top Tip 36

Involve the students

 This page may be photocopied for instructional use only. © Dave Stott (text) and Bill Stott (illustrations).

50 Top Tips for Managing Behaviour

Sarcasm or humour?

Thoughtless or supposedly humorous comments directed at a young child may seem harmless to the speaker or even funny to those listening, but to the child receiving them they can be hurtful and crushing to self-esteem and peer relationships. These types of comments can be quite damaging and the effect can last with the child for many years.

Almost every adult who has been through the education system will be able to recall an incident with a teacher that has remained in their memory ever since. In some cases the incident will have been something pleasant that enthused or motivated them. In others, the upset or discomfort they experienced at the time may never go away. What was perhaps intended as a simple 'throw-away' comment in fact produced strong, intense and lasting emotions well into adulthood.

There has been a recent tendency in both mainstream and alternative humour to highlight the out-of-the-ordinary or pick on the unusual and the non-conformist, using words to ridicule and belittle. This can seem amusing to the audience or persons not on the receiving end, and can even make the speaker feel clever, quick witted and in control. It is, however, not acceptable in a teaching and learning environment. Teachers are role models for appropriate behaviour – self-esteem and empathy are considered on equal terms in the taught curriculum – and personal comments that involve other family members, for instance, should be assiduously avoided.

Consider these examples: 'You're just like your brother, I taught him last year, and he never listened either' and 'How did you get past bonfire night dressed like that?' Both these remarks are designed to cause hilarity amongst the rest of the class at the expense of the target student. They are wholly inappropriate and demonstrate a complete lack of empathy with the student concerned.

Teachers who use these techniques as part of their behaviour management strategy are attempting to get their own needs met at the expense of others. Far from resolving issues, this approach creates an environment in which children will be fearful of being picked on, reluctant to speak or, worse still, confrontational and challenging. It demonstrates a lack of understanding about how to nurture self-esteem and motivation, and how to develop empathy in a social environment.

It is important to remind all teaching staff working with young people that no matter what the circumstance:

- The teacher is the leader in the classroom.
- The teacher is the role model.

- Behaviour not only can be taught, but also can be 'caught'. It is therefore vital that teachers' verbal and non-verbal behaviour is, at all times, appropriate and acceptable.

Before making a statement, giving a direction or issuing a reprimand, teachers should ask themselves: 'If that was my child, would I want her to be spoken to in that manner?'

Clearly, many teachers find themselves in situations that do not allow time for careful and well-prepared actions. However spontaneous, though, teachers' actions and comments should always be totally professional, with due consideration being given to the following five areas highlighted in the Social and Emotional Aspects of Learning (SEAL) materials:

1 Be aware of self feelings.
2 Develop the skills and ability to manage these feelings.
3 Be motivated.
4 Demonstrate empathy.
5 Apply the above in a social environment.

20 YEARS AGO, YOU CALLED ME A LITTLE TWERP. FANCY ANOTHER GO?

 This page may be photocopied for instructional use only. © Dave Stott (text) and Bill Stott (illustrations).

Tip 38

Emotional damage can be long lasting

It is not only the comments and phrases intended to be funny that can cause short- and long-term damage. If children are regularly told that they are hopeless or useless, or if comments such as 'Come on slowcoach, we need a calendar not a stopwatch' are regularly used, they will indeed eventually see themselves as the slowest or the worst in the class. In some cases this can be reinforced time and time again by the class teacher or, in a higher school, by every teacher who sees the student during the day or week. Think about the damage this constant repetition is doing to the student's self-esteem and how much it leaves the student open to the same name-calling by fellow classmates.

There is no intention here to attempt to create a classroom or school environment without humour. Such a place would be very sad indeed. Rather, the intention is to allow both students and adults alike to think about what they are saying, how they say it and what effect their words will have on the recipient and all those within earshot. Remember here that:

- The first person who needs to calm down is the teacher.
- Thoughts and actions produce powerful emotions.
- The feeling or emotion produced in a young person may outlast that particular lesson by many years.

Be funny, not clever

P This page may be photocopied for instructional use only. © Dave Stott (text) and Bill Stott (illustrations).

Seeking help

In the current educational environment the so-called 'myth of the good teacher' has become a dinosaur from the past. It is no longer a case of 'I can manage all situations and students on my own, I do not need any advice or help.' The development of the emotionally literate workplace encourages everyone to recognise, understand and share their feelings whilst also being aware of and empathising with colleagues' emotions. This does not preclude the fact that teachers still need to seek help, and systems should be in place to enable this to happen.

There are many situations in the daily life of a school where help or assistance is required. At these times, pushing a panic button without a system in place may be too late. Problems that arise could be related to extreme behaviour or a medical emergency and in these situations well-practised and robust systems are essential. In these cases, time and reliability are of the essence.

Just hoping that a responsible student can find a member of staff – who may or may not be free to attend – is likely to prove unsatisfactory. On the other hand, the school may have systems in place such as red cards, phone messaging or, in some situations, panic alarms. The success of such systems relies on a number of issues:

- the message actually reaching the right person
- the receiving colleague understanding the urgent nature of the message: red cards or panic messages should mean 'Come immediately – do not finish your coffee, conversation or phone call'
- the recipient of the message knowing who has sent it
- The student taking the message being well practised and knowing what is expected of them.

There are so many variables that if all the points listed above are not in place, the required help or assistance may fail to arrive on time, if at all. This is where risk assessments in the teaching and learning environment come into their own. A good starting point is the commercially available behaviour tracking software that collects information on how many times help is requested, identifies hotspots and notes individual members of staff requiring assistance. However, this information does not become effective until it has been in active use for some time.

Systems should be school-wide, understood and agreed upon by all members of staff. If using a red card system with students as messengers, make sure of the following:

- that the student knows where they are going and the name of the member of staff on the card
- that the requesting teacher's name is also on the red card
- that all staff must understand that the red card means that help is required urgently
- that the system is kept simple by having just three coloured cards, with different meanings and levels of priority
- that support staff know exactly how to act on the contents of the card – they must also be part of the system and know how to offer help.

P This page may be photocopied for instructional use only. © Dave Stott (text) and Bill Stott (illustrations).

A risk assessment should be undertaken to identify needs. This will take account of existing technology, such as internal phone systems, electronic registration, on-call systems, and so on. If the assessment identifies the need for new purchases, this must be balanced against existing or future budgets.

Other systems can also be put in place that will not necessarily involve extra budgeting and, as such, can be implemented immediately:

- Name key staff who can be allocated to specific subject or year group areas.
- Have a rota of permanent on call-staff with deputies in place if there are absences.
- Develop privately understood signals between staff, which may also include scripted responses when a member of staff identifies when help is necessary.

No loss of face

It is sometimes difficult just to impose help on people with the statement 'I see you need help ...' The member of staff concerned may reject the offer of help on the basis of, for example, being seen to lose face. The scripted response may then be 'I see you need extra help'. The key word in the second response is 'extra'. This means that the helping member of staff has identified that help is indeed required and the teacher must accept this help even though they may think it unnecessary.

When teachers are supervising students whilst they are off the school site – for example, on educational visits, work experience, and so on – the risk assessment should show that all supervising adults require visible identification badges. Many members of staff take students on school trips without any form of visible identification. Identification badges should be clear and easily understandable, showing the teacher's name, school and professional job title. These badges provide vital information for anyone providing assistance and simplify communication when help is sought.

The myth of the good teacher has finally come to an end. Like everyone else, teachers sometimes need help. They should be prepared to ask for it and to accept assistance when the situation demands this. With a system in place that is clear to all and consistently applied, there is no risk of shame or loss of face when calling on others.

TopTip39

Never reject help

 This page may be photocopied for instructional use only. © Dave Stott (text) and Bill Stott (illustrations).

Self-calming techniques

Central to effective behaviour or anger management strategies is, firstly, an ability to recognise the triggers and emotional build-up. The second and perhaps most difficult stage is to develop successful techniques to manage these emotions. The triggers can be quite varied and depend very much on the individual concerned. For example:

- how a particular situation is perceived by the individual, linked to that person's own experience
- the individual's current emotional state
- what the perceived outcome may be
- the influence of other people and the immediate environment.

Whatever the outside triggers or influences, it is people's own thoughts and feelings that are the ultimate drivers of their behaviour. It is important for both adults and students to understand these drivers in each other and to have sufficiently well-developed and practised responses to manage them.

When faced with a confrontational situation, the immediate reaction is one of 'fight or flight'. This is a natural human response (as discussed earlier in Tip 35), which is intended to protect people from possible danger

or injury. Although it may be natural, it is not necessarily the most appropriate reaction for a teaching and learning environment. It falls to teachers, in this situation, not only to develop the skills to calm themselves down, to think and behave rationally, but also to teach these skills to the students in their care. There seems little point in expecting students to be able to manage their emotions and to calm down, if teachers do not possess the ability to control their own emotions.

Teachers often work in difficult and trying situations with challenging students, where their patience is tested to the limit. They can get to the point where they either lose control completely or at least become aware that their behaviour is out of character and quite unacceptable. Most people have experienced the 'red mist' that seems to come from nowhere, and they find themselves shouting, sweating, their heart pounding, and perhaps worst of all, saying or doing things that, upon reflection, are absolutely 'over the top'.

Take the following example: 'RIGHT! YEAR 8, I am absolutely sick and tired of your behaviour. You're really getting to me and if one more person steps out of line, you're all in detention next Tuesday! OK?' The loudness, anger, sweating and out-of-control emotion that

P This page may be photocopied for instructional use only. © Dave Stott (text) and Bill Stott (illustrations).

accompany this outburst can be felt just by reading it. How might it feel to the students who are on the receiving end?

By the time this stage has been reached, it is usually too late. So before arriving at it, teachers need to be able to read and recognise the clues their bodies are giving them in the form of triggers, and to have a range of responses they can call on that will help to calm both themselves and the situation. This is where self-calming techniques come into play.

There is no point in expecting all of the following advice to be successful all the time. Everybody is an individual and what works for one person in a given situation may not work for another. Teachers and students alike need to collect together sufficient tools and strategies to create a wide menu of responses from which to choose when faced with pressure or confrontation. Many teachers and students have toolboxes filled with a wide variety of response strategies and are able to manage their own behaviour quite appropriately. Unfortunately, there are still a large number of adults and students who have toolboxes that contain only hammers.

An instinctive response

The following tips are intended to be a reminder of skills already possessed that are sometimes overlooked or forgotten. They need to be practised regularly so that the chosen response styles or self-calming techniques become instinctive and the first and preferred choice.

- Deep breathing not only allows teachers to focus on something other than the confrontation, but also provides the essential extra oxygen to counteract the adrenalin rush associated with threat. Try breathing in for two seconds through the nose and then breathing out for three seconds through the mouth.

- For many people, counting is an effective calming measure. Try counting upwards – counting down may mean a blast-off when zero is reached.

- Relax. Think about the non-verbal messages. Tension in the neck, arms and face will add to the pressurised feeling.

- Open the palms, face them downwards or put hands together in front of the body. Unclench those fists!

- Stand slightly sideways to the student. Put the body weight on the back foot, rather than leaning towards the other person.

- Consider, physically and/or mentally, moving away from the source of agitation. There may be no need to be that close. Create some personal space.

- Catch the eye of another adult in the room, or spot a student who is not a cause of annoyance, and exchange glances.

With regular practice these techniques will become an instinctive and effective response. Don't wait until they are needed, because in a pressurised situation they will not be there.

Top Tip 40

Practise the techniques

 This page may be photocopied for instructional use only. © Dave Stott (text) and Bill Stott (illustrations).

Sent out

Many students have been sent out of the classroom where they spend the next 10, 20 or 30 minutes either celebrating that they are no longer part of the lesson they hate or causing major upsets in all parts of the school. Quite a few students have spent a fair percentage of their school life in the corridor and for some this is where they prefer to be.

If leaving the classroom is a sanction that is an agreed part of a behaviour plan, it is important that the plan is revisited in order to consider the following points:

- At what point in the plan does 'leave the room' occur?
- Where does the student go once they have left the room?
- How long does the consequence last? Until they calm down? Show some remorse? When they promise to behave? For good?
- Are any other members of the teaching staff involved?
- How is the 'leave the room' sanction initiated? Is it shouted? Is it a calm statement? Is the behaviour support team sent for?
- What happens if the student refuses?
- What is the intended benefit of excluding the student from the room?

It is difficult to see how a teacher can maintain their duty of care to a student who is no longer in their classroom, nor is it clear how exclusion from the class will improve the future behaviour of the targeted student. Simply sending the student out of the room will achieve only two things for certain: the student will no longer be disturbing the class and they won't be annoying the teacher. These points should, however, be kept in mind, because part of a teacher's responsibility is to provide a teaching and learning environment that allows teachers to teach and provides all students with an equal opportunity to learn and interact on an acceptable social level. The chronic misbehaviour and disruptive influence of one or more individuals does not make for an acceptable learning environment.

If it is decided within the school that 'sending out' is an acceptable sanction, it is worth considering the following practical suggestions to ensure that this particular consequence is going to have a successful outcome. Without careful planning, teachers may find themselves appearing on all the tracking systems used by the school which reveal that students are continually out of their classroom and causing endless disruption to other classrooms and teachers.

P This page may be photocopied for instructional use only. © Dave Stott (text) and Bill Stott (illustrations).

The six-point plan

Firstly, the school should decide whether sending a student out of the classroom is a sanction that is acceptable. If it is, or becomes, part of the agreed discipline plan, then the following should be considered:

1   Ensure that all responses to inappropriate behaviour are clearly structured. Teachers and students should be absolutely clear at which point the 'leave the room' sanction is implemented. For example, it may be decided to operate a five- or six-point response to difficult behaviour. Leaving the room would clearly be used only as a fairly high-level sanction after, say, levels one to four (or five) have been used. Inconsistent application of this sanction will provoke a sense of unfairness, so all students must face the same menu of sanctions.

2   Where will the student go when they leave the room? Simply going out into the corridor unsupervised and with the whole school building easily accessible is not acceptable. Try teaming up with another teacher in the same year group, faculty or department. If a student needs to leave the room, they should be sent to a 'partner' class. This could potentially lead to chaos, however, if too many students are sent out of the class and constantly moved from one room to another. If this system is to work, students should be sent to a class group of similar age. Sending a Year 5 child to a Year 1 group will simply result in humiliation and ridicule, which in the long run could hardly be regarded as an appropriate behaviour management technique.

3   How long will the student be out of the room? It is tempting to leave some students out of the room until the end of the lesson. The 'worst case scenario' is that the student is out of sight and therefore out of mind. The reason for using any sanction is to stop inappropriate behaviour and allow the student to make a better choice next time. It is not to give the teacher a period of light relief or devolve the responsibility to a colleague for an indefinite period.

4   What will the student be doing whilst out of the room? The simple answer is that an appropriate activity should be given to the excluded student even when they are joining another class group.

5   Any exclusion from the room should be on a clear and agreed timed basis. It is important for the student and teacher alike to understand that the student will be returning to the room as soon as possible.

6   Teachers should ensure that they have effective back-up systems in place (such as a behaviour support team or the services of teaching/non-teaching colleagues) should they have difficulty in carrying out the agreed strategy.

TopTip41

Out of sight but not out of mind

 This page may be photocopied for instructional use only. © Dave Stott (text) and Bill Stott (illustrations).

Serotonin time

Serotonin, first discovered in 1948, is a substance found extensively in the human gut, as well as in the blood stream. In the human body it is synthesised from the amino acid tryptophan by various enzymes. A tiny amount of the substance can have a huge impact on behaviour. Imbalances are linked, for example, to mood swings, emotional state, sleeping patterns and appetite.

One of a teacher's many tasks is to create a working environment that enables students to feel secure, both physically and emotionally. When they are relaxed and engaged with the learning process, serotonin is naturally released in the brain, leading to greater cognitive awareness and sharper reflexes. It is at this point that students can adopt a style and behaviour where learning is at its most effective. Teachers should try to establish some 'serotonin time' during a lesson – a time specifically designed to affect mood, focus the group and act as a catalyst for some concentrated work.

How, then, can serotonin time be created in the classroom? There is a generic requirement to provide an environment that is stimulating and interesting. It should be physically safe and secure. The teacher's delivery style should be reflective of the individual learning needs of the students. Within these demands the teacher should be creating opportunities to affect the mood and emotions of the entire class group positively. The sterile orderly classroom, which focuses entirely on the curriculum and learning outcomes, is not necessarily the most interesting, stimulating and exciting place

to be. On the other hand, it is not the intention to promote a teaching and learning environment in which the teacher must also be an entertainer. The approach is to identify periods of time during each lesson that are specifically aimed at having a positive influence on the emotions of both teacher and student.

The starting point for teachers is to identify their own emotional state each day when they arrive at work. How does this rate on a scale of 1 to 10, with 10 being fantastic and 1 just dreadful? If the mood that morning is really terrible, consider making a real effort at leaving any emotional baggage at the school gate and stepping into the school grounds with a positive plan:

• Make a positive comment or statement to a work colleague or student each day.

• Make a note of how many similar comments are received from colleagues or students (this is about giving and receiving).

• Encourage students to do the same to both members of staff and peers.

• Have a positive influence on the mood of colleagues and students.

Some students, and indeed members of staff, will need opportunities to practise giving appropriate comments whilst also developing skills such as active communication, maintaining eye contact, sincerity and adopting a positive body language.

P This page may be photocopied for instructional use only. © Dave Stott (text) and Bill Stott (illustrations).

Tip 42

Introduce the 'feel-good factor'

When it comes to lesson time, consider how the learning and active engagement of students can be enhanced through the use of serotonin time. If the lesson is one long period of entertainment, it will inevitably lead to off-task behaviour and a complete misunderstanding of the teacher's intentions. Plan the lesson carefully so that it is punctuated with timed and structured opportunities for restoring interest levels and when the 'feel-good factor' has a direct influence on the main task in hand:

- Be prepared to use timed interruptions or breaks during the lesson (approximately every 20 minutes) that lighten the mood. A brief video clip or a one-off change of activity for one or two minutes can be highly stimulating and productive.

- Show-and-tell sessions in the primary classroom could be structured in such a way that they become brief interjections throughout the day, rather than crowded together first thing in the morning.

- Use the staffroom to practise serotonin time with colleagues.

- Send encouraging notes home with students, hand out stickers and make telephone calls. These positive activities can produce incredibly powerful serotonin times for parents, thus raising self-esteem and creating strong partnerships.

The intention should not be to make lessons disjointed, with all manner of interruptions. Assess the use of serotonin time carefully, so that it fulfils the primary aims of improving the learning environment and enhancing the emotional state of students. People learn and respond when they feel good – positive attitudes and approaches will help the development of emotional literacy in all students and improve their life chances beyond school.

Top Tip 42

Positive inputs = positive results

 This page may be photocopied for instructional use only. © Dave Stott (text) and Bill Stott (illustrations).

Speaking and listening skills

'In one ear and out of the other' is something frequently said about students in the classroom. Teachers will recognise this just as they will the classroom chatterboxes who continually demonstrate their conversational skills with colleagues. These same students are often those who have developed highly selective listening skills, choosing to hear comments on which they wish to act (such as 'time to go home') and ignoring those that they cannot be bothered to deal with ('Sorry teacher, I didn't hear you').

Learning to listen, and speaking at the appropriate time, are life skills that should be learned in the home and reinforced at school. But how many students never develop these skills as youngsters and, as a result, display the following inappropriate behaviours as adults?

- Failing to engage eye contact
- not physically engaging with others during a conversation (that is, not facing the person they are speaking with, or turning away during a conversation)
- too intent on getting their point across rather than listening to what is being said
- continually talking over another person, not understanding that they need to take turns in a conversation
- trying to outdo their conversation partner with their responses, causing anxiety and perhaps confrontation (that is, always 'trumping' an experience three times over)
- constantly changing the subject, being much happier to talk about their own agenda rather than a shared topic

- giving no clues as to whether they are either listening or have even understood what has been said
- failing to demonstrate any empathy in their replies or comments.

Behaviours such as these develop over a long time: they begin in childhood. This is why teachers need to create opportunities for students to practise appropriate skills in the classroom, and to model these skills to students on a regular, day-to-day basis. This will enable students to develop the skills for themselves, so that good speaking and listening become natural and automatic response mechanisms, which they can carry with them for the rest of their lives.

Before setting out to teach new skills or modify ones that already exist, it is important to understand that everyone has different techniques and mannerisms, depending on the environment, cultural norms and the specific situation. For example, most people have a particular telephone 'voice' they use when they do not know who is calling. People also draw on different skills for different occasions, such as when they are with friends, meeting someone for the first time or at a job interview.

To find out the basic communication styles that students already possess, try setting up some role-play situations that will allow them to demonstrate these. These situations might include:

- mock interviews with and without preset questions
- informal chat sessions discussing topics of their choice
- formal discussion on a preset topic

P This page may be photocopied for instructional use only. © Dave Stott (text) and Bill Stott (illustrations).

- practical aural and oral sessions followed by simple questions relating to content and understanding of a sessions' topic.

Most people do not see themselves in the way they are seen by others. The use of audio and video recording can prove invaluable here. Before carrying out any such recording, however, it is important to obtain the necessary permissions from management, parents and students.

Active listening skills

Once a baseline regarding existing skills and competencies has been established, those skills that are not so well developed can be addressed. The first list of bullet points above gives some indication of common communication deficiencies, which can be used as a starting point. Take into account the type of students involved and cater for all styles of learning: visual, auditory and kinetic. Identify the individual skill in each student that needs development and provide a formal taught lesson as well as later opportunities to practise. The following four steps are good indicators of active listening and can be used as an exercise:

1   using eye contact
2   allowing the speaker to complete a sentence or contribution before replying
3   indicating to the speaker that they are being heard and understood, either by using head movements (nodding) or by making short verbal comments ('yes' or 'I see')
4   making sure that the reply relates to the subject of the conversation.

Try some less formal activities to liven up the learning experience. The following Just a Minute activity is often popular with students and is an enjoyable way of developing listening and speaking skills.

One person tries to speak on a given topic for one minute, but must not hesitate, deviate from the subject or repeat any words. When successfully challenged, the challenger must continue the subject under the same guidelines and try to complete the minute. This game requires quick thinking, clear speaking and careful listening.

Top Tip 43

Maintain eye contact with students

P This page may be photocopied for instructional use only. © Dave Stott (text) and Bill Stott (illustrations).

50 Top Tips
for Managing Behaviour

Systems and routines

Teachers should never make the assumption that academic, everyday and special occasion behaviours were all taught by the students' previous teacher. Forget what may or may not have happened before. Students need the clarity and guidance of their new teacher so that they know what is expected of them from the very first day. It is possible for the Year 2 teacher to assume that the new class were taught how to enter their room and sit down quietly during their time in Year 1. If the assumption is incorrect and that particular skill was either not taught or not completely absorbed, it is possible that some children will transfer into secondary education still not possessing the necessary skills to survive in the classroom.

Without these basic skills some students can find it extremely difficult to meet the expectations of the various subject teachers. Unhelpful and often hurtful remarks may be directed at those students who are struggling to comply. It is not uncommon for students to receive comments such as 'What on earth did they teach you at that school?' or 'You may have behaved like that last year, but in my classroom things are very different.'

The teacher is the role model and leader in the classroom and has the wider responsibility for helping all students to understand and comply with classroom and school systems. Some of these students may have been struggling for many months to make sense of a wide range of academic requirements: behavioural expectations are another layer on top of their classroom work and for many this is a lot to take on. Therefore, do not expect students to conform immediately; behaviour must be taught, understood and practised regularly just like any other part of the curriculum. At regular intervals notice and comment on those students who follow the agreed rules and routines and use positive peer pressure to encourage those who may be slow to comply.

There should not be a robotic-like conformity throughout the school: individuality and personality are important too. Teachers should set out clearly their own expectations, teaching their own systems and consistently applying them within the framework of the school's overall policies.

It is also worth taking some time to think about the number of instructions that students receive in the course of a lesson or a whole day. Make certain that those who receive these instructions understand them, are able to carry them out and are not overwhelmed. Almost all these directions fit into one of three general categories:

1 academic: usually the requirements of individual subjects; for example, writing the date, underlining, setting out a piece of writing, which book to use

2 general activities: such as entering and leaving a classroom, attracting the teacher's attention, seating plans, noise levels in the classroom, answering the register

3 special activities: for example, how to behave when a visitor is in the classroom, whilst on out-of-school visits, during a fire drill.

Not all at once

For many students these and many more instructions are piled upon them on the first day or in the first week of the academic year or term. Very few of them – with the exception of the fire drill – are reinforced and practised on a regular basis. These instructions need to be repeated regularly – not just when students fail to comply. All school and classroom systems and routines should be taught, referred to and reinforced whenever possible. One way to reinforce some of these is by using classroom posters so that there is a permanent reminder to hand.

Another is in the way that students are praised or acknowledged. Do not say just 'Good' or 'Well done'; instead, refer to why the student being addressed is being recognised: 'Good, you raised your hand to answer', 'Well done, you've put your things away neatly.' This positive reinforcement technique rewards the student whilst at the same time reminding the whole class of the routines, systems and expected behaviour. It is therefore important to:

- teach these systems and routines in the same way as curriculum subjects
- check that all students understand
- practise the routines regularly throughout the year
- supplement the teaching with visual reminders around the school or classroom
- be consistent: if there is any need to change systems, go through the same teaching process as for changes that are made in other areas.

Finally, teachers quite often say that they like to change the routines in the classroom on a regular basis to ensure that students listen and are kept motivated – that this takes the routine boredom out of the day. But does it? It may well be true for a minority of students, but many cannot manage constant change and become confused and disengaged. This is when general behaviour can begin to deteriorate.

TopTip 44

Don't change for the sake of change

P This page may be photocopied for instructional use only. © Dave Stott (text) and Bill Stott (illustrations).

50 Top Tips for Managing Behaviour

Tactical ignoring

Tactical ignoring is a useful strategy that can be used when responding to certain challenging behaviours that are displayed simply as a means of gaining attention. It is a useful skill for teachers to develop because it avoids being reeled into situations that really do not justify the amount of time that may otherwise be spent on dealing with them.

Students should always be given time to comply with instructions. Many adults simply do not give young people sufficient time to respond to requests. This can lead the teacher to invading the student's personal space, repeating the instruction louder than is really necessary and then remaining in the same space, waiting for the student to comply. The waiting time is often too short. Repeating the instruction and raising the voice within the space of a few seconds will invariably lead to a negative or, at worst, a confrontational response.

When students are faced with an unending torrent of directions and requests, they too unwittingly employ

tactical ignoring as a strategy. Teachers normally refer to this as 'in one ear and out of the other', but it often happens because students feel deluged and that they are not being given sufficient time to comply. On those occasions when sufficient time is not made available and a student begins to play up, the teacher's attention may well switch from the primary instruction and initial behaviour to any unwanted extra, or secondary, behaviour. These situations can deteriorate rapidly.

Here's an example: Teacher: 'John turn round and get on with your work.' John did turn round but his compliance with the instruction was accompanied by a scowl and muttering under his breath. Teacher (again): 'Don't you look at me like that, young man, and what was that you said?' Here, the situation could quickly develop into an argument with both teacher and John feeling that they were not being listened to or treated with respect. There was no recognition by the teacher that John did actually comply with the initial instruction. The focus of the continued dialogue was on the negative aspects of

P This page may be photocopied for instructional use only. © Dave Stott (text) and Bill Stott (illustrations).

John's behaviour. Although the scowl and muttering under the breath cannot be totally ignored, a risk assessment was clearly needed:

- Did the teacher's immediate reaction to John's behaviour make the situation worse?
- Was the teacher remaining calm?
- Did John comply with the original request?
- Are there any other suitable strategies that could have been used to keep the interaction low key but still allow John to comply with the request?

Further techniques can be drawn on in order to achieve the desired result. It is important to teach compliance with instructions together with the appropriate associated behaviour. The teacher's job, as the role model, is to allow the student time and to be clear about the behaviour that is expected in the classroom. When giving direct instructions, keep the following points in mind:

- Move in towards the student, using their first name to gain attention.
- Remember the student's personal space and be aware of the body language used when giving the instruction.
- Make a clear and specific statement of what is required.
- Once the instruction has been given, the body language should demonstrate clearly that the teacher is moving away and that there is an expectation that the student will comply.
- Never remain in the student's space waiting for compliance. Negative body language (folded arms, foot tapping and direct eye contact) will only make the situation worse.
- Ignore any short delay that may occur before the student complies.
- Do not totally ignore non-compliance or give the student too long to respond. This sends the wrong message and the student will feel empowered to ignore future instructions.

Tactical ignoring as a conscious decision

Moving away from the student allows the teacher to practise the next stage in tactical ignoring:

- Be aware of the secondary behaviours that are often linked to reluctant compliance.
- Make a considered decision about whether this secondary behaviour can be tactically ignored at that precise moment.
- Be prepared to return to the student once they have complied with the initial instruction and remind them of how and why they are expected to comply.

This is how it could work: John complies with the instruction as above, but still displays a scowl and mutters under his breath. The teacher moves away after giving the instruction (two or three paces is sufficient), ignores the scowl and muttering, and rewards the compliance, 'Good. Well done for getting back on with your work.' A little later the teacher returns when the student is calm to remind him of his unwanted behaviour: 'John, it is good that you are getting back on with your work, but I can't let you answer back, giving me bad looks.' In this example the teacher tactically ignored the behavioural response in order to start a low-key dialogue and establish a 'win-win' situation. The student could be gently reminded at the end of the lesson that his behaviour was inappropriate.

Tactical ignoring is not a sanction

 This page may be photocopied for instructional use only. © Dave Stott (text) and Bill Stott (illustrations).

Teaching assistants

Teaching assistant, classroom assistant, higher level teaching assistant (HLTA), behaviour support assistant, parent helper and learning support assistant are just some of the posts that have appeared in schools over the last few years. Some of these posts have caused confusion for teachers, parents and students alike. The role of the support worker and the perceived hierarchy in the classroom are often difficult to understand and are often ill-explained. The following are just some of the ways in which teaching assistants are perceived:

- an extra adult who is there to prepare materials, put up displays, listen to readers
- a person who is assigned to a specific student who has been identified as having special educational needs
- a highly skilled and well-qualified adult who forms an effective partnership working alongside the teacher.

The teacher who feels uncertain of or threatened by the presence of another adult in the classroom, will invariably under-use that person's skills, fail to form an effective working relationship with them and, in the process, confuse students. Students who are confused will test boundaries and exploit inconsistencies between staff members. If a teacher feels negative about their assistant, this is certain to be picked up by the students and lead to a breakdown in behaviour.

It is not unusual for a classroom assistant to be appointed to the role following a reply to an advertisement in a local newspaper, and then to find themselves in the classroom with little or no induction, training or even an introduction to the teacher. For assistants working in secondary schools, this can be seriously challenging and alarming. Being assigned to a student experiencing difficulties in school, and faced with the prospect of trying to work with up to a dozen different teachers in a week, can be a daunting experience. It can challenge even the most self-confident of people.

As a newly appointed member of staff, an assistant would not usually choose to cause problems or upset relationships by asking for a clear and relevant job description. Inexperienced people are unlikely to ask for planning and meeting time on their personal timetable. Consequently, many assistants learn the role whilst actually carrying it out, often by trial and error.

The first thing any teaching assistant needs is an agreed job description, which must also be seen by the teachers with whom they work. A generic job description and person specification for all support staff within the school

should be available; this can then be personalised for the specific role the assistant will be undertaking. It is vital that communication takes place at all levels and that all concerned know the teaching assistant's exact role:

- within the school
- within the classroom/faculty/subject area
- with the group or individual student.

Once these areas have been established, it is important that time is formally set aside for teacher and assistant to communicate. Top of the priority list in these discussions must be to confirm the teacher's ground rules and boundaries within the classroom. The teaching assistant should become familiar with the reward and consequence systems and know how they are implemented. There is often a real, or sometimes a perceived, adult hierarchy within the classroom, and regular communication with agreed responsibilities will reduce any confusion or tension that may arise out of misunderstandings.

The teaching assistant must be treated as a valued member of staff. This includes being provided with somewhere to store their resources and possessions, for example. Comfort zones contribute to the teaching assistant's morale and will undoubtedly affect their performance. If the assistant is to work regularly with the same teacher or group of teachers, ensure that lines of communication, such as emails, message boards or even an exercise book, remain open and accessible.

Depending on the working environment of the teaching assistant, it is important that they are familiar with the working practices of all the teachers involved. Where difficulties arise it is also important for the assistant to be clear about line management. Who do they speak to when things go wrong? Who is responsible for their professional development?

Beneficial for students

The relationship between teacher and teaching assistant, when working well, provides the students with many benefits:

- Behaviour in the classroom is managed by two adults, who seem to have an uncanny understanding of each other.
- Challenging situations can be calmed and resolved at the lowest level. Just catching the eye of the teacher is sometimes enough to take the edge off an incident.

 This page may be photocopied for instructional use only. © Dave Stott (text) and Bill Stott (illustrations).

- Contact with more adults in the classroom gives students the opportunity to learn more skills.

It would be excellent if, as part of their in-service training for teachers, schools were to include sessions on how to work with teaching assistants. Good practice in establishing an emotionally literate school should involve all stakeholders in school development plans. Teachers, teaching assistants and all support staff should be included in this process.

Top Tip 46

Involve teaching assistants at all levels

P This page may be photocopied for instructional use only. © Dave Stott (text) and Bill Stott (illustrations).

Timed reminders

For many students just simply 'getting through' the hour-long lesson can be a major issue. Anxiety or even foreboding can begin at the start of the week, sometimes even on the way to school on the first day. It is true to say that some students may well be preparing themselves for disruption, confrontation or exclusion from the lesson before the classroom is even reached. This negative approach to the day can often result in challenging or off-task behaviour.

Teachers will have prepared and differentiated the content of the lesson and know exactly what they want to achieve by the end of the period. Inevitably, the lesson will be made up of a variety of activities that may include:

- entering the room, welcome and settling in period
- spoken introduction
- direct teaching to whole group and/or individuals
- quiet study/writing time
- question-and-answer session
- review and evaluation
- clearing up and end of lesson
- leaving the room.

Most teachers will be aware of how much time is allocated to each of the segments listed above and students will also know, from experience, how long each takes. Some students, such as those who have come to school in a negative frame of mind, will choose not to be concerned with timing. They will spend much of their time off task, chatting or generally being disruptive, and do not possess the skills to apply a structure to their work schedule. These students will certainly need the teacher's help in prompting and organisational skills.

Assisting them with a structure, reminding them and preparing them for changes in the activities will not just help them remain on task, but will allow teachers to be proactive in their behaviour management techniques. Constant reminders to stop talking, sit down, get back to work, and so on, may cause more disruption than the initial off-task behaviour. Clear timings, forewarning of changes in activities and positive recognition can be, in this situation, a powerful behaviour management tool.

Whilst the actual timing for the whole lesson is generally fully understood by all, it is important that the separate activities are broken down into clear time slots, and this should be made obvious to the students. Setting out the lesson in a format similar to a timed agenda will give a clear indication of expectations to all students.

Many younger students will find a visual reminder very helpful in planning a structure to their work. An egg timer, a buzzer or an electronic timing device with a clear visual read-out allows the students to understand not only what is expected of them, but also how long they are allowed for the activity. Gauging time can be a very difficult skill for many children. Mentally judging five, 10 or 15 minutes can prove to be almost impossible for some, so it will be hopeless to expect them to structure their work over a whole lesson. This will merely lead to arguments and overall disruption.

The timed agenda

Once the content of the lesson has been prepared, carefully plan the associated timings. These should be communicated to all the students, in an age-appropriate manner, using clear start and end procedures. Remember to include reminders and warnings of changes in activities. Use the following as a basis for future lesson plans:

- At the start of an activity, give a clear indication of how much time is allowed for a particular piece of work.
- Use a visual timing device for younger students; have a clock in the room for older students.

 This page may be photocopied for instructional use only. © Dave Stott (text) and Bill Stott (illustrations).

- Give a five-minute warning and then a one-minute warning for all changes in activities. Try saying 'I'm going to stop you in one minute to talk about …' rather than simply saying 'Right, everyone, stop and listen.' Some students will be absorbed in the activity and will not want to stop immediately, whilst others will not even have started and will need a reminder to get back on task.

- Use the same warning system for the end of the lessons; give clear and advanced warnings.

- Allow time for any questions, and for clearing up and preparing to leave the room. Remember that the next group or member of staff will not thank anyone for leaving a room in a terrible state.

When making allowances for individual students, it is also worthwhile considering varying the timings. Break up a 60-minute session into five, 10, 15 or 20 segments, rather than six 10-minute activities, to allow for flexibility. For the student who is easily bored by the prospect of an hour-long session, dividing the time into 'bite-sized pieces' will make the lesson appear to pass more quickly and will help them remain on task.

TopTip47

Small segments, not large chunks

 This page may be photocopied for instructional use only. © Dave Stott (text) and Bill Stott (illustrations).

Visibility

People form an impression of others within seconds of their first meeting. This has an enormous impact when teachers meet a new student (or vice versa) because these immediate impressions are quite difficult to alter once formed. The impression that is formed is based mainly on body language because more than 75 per cent of communication is non-verbal. Body language, image and posture all set the scene even before verbal language is used to communicate.

Most people have heard their voice played back as a recording: few people actually enjoy the experience and most feel quite uncomfortable. Some people have also seen video footage of themselves in their workplace and, once again, this can be discomforting. Considering that the view on the video and the voice on the tape represent how the individual is seen and heard by others, it is surprising that little use is made of this technology in initial teacher training or in subsequent continuing professional development activities.

Access to video and audio facilities is not always practical, but if these are available they can be very useful tools. If they are not available, colleagues can share and establish systems and ways of training that analyse their communication strategies and styles of teaching. This can be done within staff training days or as part of ongoing performance development. Given the impact that voice and non-verbal language have on the behaviour of others, honing and understanding communication skills is a vital element in managing the classroom, and it is well worth investing time and effort in this area.

Modern technology is indeed useful, although it is daunting for some. However, good, old-fashioned and robust methods of observation and clear feedback can also prove invaluable and should not be overlooked. Feedback from all stakeholders is important, but do recognise that students can be painfully honest in their observations. It is the straightforward approach that can prove most effective if a positive view is adopted and action is taken on any lessons learned. If doing these sessions in a group feels uncomfortable, work with a 'critical friend' and establish a system of observation and evaluation. Then see how some often simple changes in teacher behaviour can have a powerful effect on the behaviour of the students in the class.

Not for the faint-hearted

A variety of methods may be used to effect a change in both body and verbal language, which, as just noted, can have a positive effect on the behaviour of students:

- As mentioned, teachers could work collaboratively with a 'critical friend' to offer clear and honest observations of their communication skills. This should be based on actual classroom work whilst managing students, rather than the friend's subjective impression.

- Be brave. Try using some technological aids, such as an audio recorder for self-evaluation. Be aware of the protocols of using recording devices in the workplace and do not use them without clear and full permission. Make a critical analysis. Was the voice too loud, too shrill and too uncertain? Was it too quick or too slow? Was it confrontational? Play it to colleagues and friends and seek their opinion. Practise any changes that are needed and use the new techniques in the classroom.

- Be even braver! Use the same technology as used by sports people. Set up a camcorder to record in-class performance or ask a colleague to use one (but always remember legal and in-school protocols). This inevitably works better in a real classroom whilst teaching real students, but if this is not possible or permission is not given, set up a session with volunteers away from the classroom. What message is the body language conveying? How about the overall appearance? The intention is not to embarrass, but to allow the teacher to make a critical and yet non-threatening self-evaluation and to be seen as they are by others.

- Be braver still! Perhaps the truest test of how the teacher is seen by others is to gather comments from that ultimate user group: the students. Spend time in devising an audit or checklist system for use by the students that gathers objective comments rather than subjective criticism. Once a baseline or benchmark has been established, set some clear objectives and a time frame within which changes can be made. Measure the effectiveness of these changes and see this as an ongoing development.

Critical self-analysis can be a difficult and sometimes unnerving activity to undertake, but the benefits that arise in creating positive working relationships and acceptable behaviour from colleagues and students is more than worth the effort. Remember that the object of the exercise is for teachers to see themselves as they are seen by others, thus creating the opportunity for real and effective change.

Top Tip 48

Don't hide away

 This page may be photocopied for instructional use only. © Dave Stott (text) and Bill Stott (illustrations).

Voice matching

People can unwittingly change their voices to match the situation in which they find themselves: they use different voices in different situations. For example, a person from the north of England may spend a week or two in the south and then return to the north only to be told their voice displays a southern 'twang'. Or the voice changes when answering the telephone to an unfamiliar number, and the quiet voice is adopted in a quiet environment.

As role models for students in school, teachers should be aware of how appropriate behaviour can be 'caught' as well as taught. In an environment in which raised voices, poor listening and confrontation are the accepted modes of communication, many students will inevitably consider these to be the way to behave. Clearly, if teachers are to create emotionally literate schools and classrooms, they have a responsibility to model and practise good communication skills.

Indeed, a relaxed, quiet voice accompanied by the appropriate body language can go a long way to remaining calm and thereby defuse a potentially explosive situation. Angry, shouting students will be aware of their teacher's attitude through that teacher's voice. They will find it very difficult to continue shouting and exhibiting loud behaviour when communicating with an adult who is in complete control of themselves in both verbal and non-verbal behaviour. This also has a ripple effect on any onlookers and other class members. Watching a teacher or classroom assistant who is faced with a highly confrontational situation is considered quite a sport for some students. Their subsequent behaviour will often depend on the teacher's response to the initial confrontation.

A teacher's main aim in any confrontational situation should be to:

- remain calm
- defuse the situation, using appropriate verbal and non-verbal techniques
- maintain control
- use the opportunity to teach appropriate skills to all involved.

It is rare for anyone to hear an audio recording of their own voice and be pleased with what they hear. Because teachers use different voices as the situation demands throughout the day, work with a colleague (rather than a tape recorder), paying attention to each other's style of speaking to students. This is easier in classrooms where teachers work together with teaching assistants. At the end of the teaching day, spend some time discussing each other's voice volume and tone. Set aside some time during the week to report back to one another with observations and recommendations, not forgetting to discuss feelings when different voices were used.

Throughout this book, the key word of advice has been 'preparation'. Using the voice also falls into this category. Pre-planned, almost scripted, responses to confrontational or argumentative students are more likely to sound calm and controlled than off-the-cuff comments that may contain anger. Try the following staged approach when responding to threats or confrontation:

1 Risk assess the situation (this can happen very quickly with practice).
2 Before speaking, be aware of non-verbal language.
3 Use a calm voice and a scripted response ('John, I can see you are angry. You need to …').

Practise and keep on practising

The intention is to use a calm and calming voice and for the young person to voice match. As noted above, it is very difficult to shout at someone who is refusing to be drawn in. Practise this technique so that it becomes automatic when dealing with difficult situations. Through practice, it will be obvious how difficult it is to continue an argument with someone who is remaining calm both in body language and in voice. Do not be tempted to use voice matching in an oppositional manner. Do not fall into the trap that many angry students (or colleagues) may set by 'outshouting' them. They will expect their loud confrontational voices to be matched. This is not a conversation; it is an argument that will quickly get out of control.

In summary, teachers should:

- listen to their own recorded voice using audio equipment in the privacy of their home in order to assess how their voice sounds
- use a 'critical friend' (such as a teaching assistant) to discuss their voice technique in the classroom
- practise using a calm voice – and keep on practising
- use a scripted response
- be persistent, and not expect the young person to voice match immediately in a challenging situation
- spend time teaching appropriate responses to students, letting them experience how powerful voice matching can be
- combine a calm voice with good body language – this takes practice too.

TopTip49

Always use a calming voice

 This page may be photocopied for instructional use only. © Dave Stott (text) and Bill Stott (illustrations).

Who wants the last word?

Just reading the heading above will bring to mind immediately a particular student or, in some cases, groups of students. Simply looking at the timetable is sufficient to put many teachers and support staff into reactionary mode. It is easy for some teachers to allow themselves to be drawn into an adversarial style of arguing to try to maintain credibility. Teachers are role models and should be able to distance themselves from confrontation and use their skills to guide and help the student.

Unfortunately, not many people practise their skills in dealing with arguments. They prefer instead to rely on their ability to react to situations. When using this response style, people's natural reactions dominate and the response is emotional, not scripted. A reactive response to the student who answers back, wants the last word or is prepared to enter an argument means that the teacher:

- takes it personally
- overreacts and may become aggressive
- conversely, gives in and becomes passive
- tends to be negative
- has no plan for how to deal with the student's behaviour, and has not prepared what to say or how to say it.

Teachers, however, can manage these situations and their own emotions effectively if they employ well-rehearsed skills and strategies. These enable them to be proactive, consistent and effective. This style of response is more effective because the teacher:

- does not take it personally
- is able to remain calm and does not overreact
- is concerned about achieving a 'win-win' outcome
- knows what to say and how to say it, states clear expectations and knows what to do next. The message to the student is that the response is planned, prepared, fair and consistent.

As with all practical tips and strategies, these suggestions are not foolproof and will not necessarily be successful in every situation. To achieve the best possible chance of success, teachers should not use these strategies in isolation from anything else. Practise and think about verbal and non-verbal language, eye contact, pitch and volume of voice and proximity to the student. These are all essential elements of a successful management strategy.

P This page may be photocopied for instructional use only. © Dave Stott (text) and Bill Stott (illustrations).

A step-by-step approach

The student who intends to have the last word or is prepared to attempt to argue with the teacher will be focusing primarily on their own responses and the effect they are having on both the teacher and other students in close proximity. In this situation the teacher needs to be able to assess the problem quickly, use a well-practised self-calming technique and focus on a scripted response. These are the steps that need to be taken:

1   Move in towards the student, be aware of pace and body language. Move close enough to deliver a clear instruction, but not so close that the student's personal space is being invaded – arm's length is close enough.

2   Whenever possible, use the student's first name.

3   Now give a clear instruction stating exactly what is expected. For example: 'John, you need to stop talking and begin your work right now.' It is likely here that John will want the last word and will begin to explain why the instruction cannot be followed.

4   Use a scripted response: 'Yes I understand that, but John, you need to stop talking and begin your work right now.' This repeats the exact words that were used previously.

5   Faced with another comment from the student, repeat the same format of a statement of understanding followed by a repeat of the original instruction: 'OK, that doesn't matter at the moment, but John, you need to stop talking and begin your work right now.'

As a guide, the statement of understanding (which shows the student they are actually being listened to), followed by the repeat instruction, is most likely to succeed when used no more than three times. Used four, five or more times, it is probably not going to work in this instance; the student may have worked out the teacher's strategy.

Delivered in a calming and scripted manner, remembering all the verbal and non-verbal points, this strategy is very powerful and highly effective. It does, however, need to be practised and to be part of the natural and everyday professional response to a verbal confrontation.

Top Tip 50

Scripted responses work – reaction inflames

 This page may be photocopied for instructional use only. © Dave Stott (text) and Bill Stott (illustrations).

References

Canter L & Canter M, 1992, *Assertive Discipline for Secondary School Educators*, Canter, Santa Monica, CA.

Faupel A (ed), 2003, *Emotional Literacy: Assessment and Intervention Ages 11–16*, nferNelson, London.

Loggerhead Films, 2008, DVDs: *Interactive Skills, Managing Chronic Behaviour Problems, Managing Severe and Acute Behaviour,* http://www.loggerheadfilms.co.uk

Social and Emotional Aspects of Learning (SEAL) website: http://www.standards.dcsf.gov.uk/nationalstrategies